Navigating the Sermon

Lent and Easter Seasons Edition for Cycle C
of the Revised Common Lectionary

A Compilation of "Charting the Course" Columns from
Emphasis: A Preaching Journal for the Parish Pastor
a Component of **SermonSuite.com**

CSS Publishing Company, Inc.
Lima, Ohio

NAVIGATING THE SERMON
LENT AND EASTER SEASONS EDITION, CYCLE C

FIRST EDITION
Copyright © 2013
by CSS Publishing Co., Inc.

Scripture quotations are from the New Revised Standard Version of the Bible. Copyright 1989 by the Division of Christian Education of the National Council of the Churches of Christ in the USA. Used by permission.

Some scripture quotations marked RSV are from the Revised Standard Version of the Bible, copyrighted 1946, 1952 ©, 1971, 1973, by the Division of Christian Education of the National Council of the Churches of Christ in the USA. Used by permission.

Some scripture quotations marked NIV are taken from the Holy Bible, New International Version. Copyright © 1973, 1978, 1984 International Bible Society. Used by permission of Zondervan Bible Publishers. All rights reserved.

For more information about CSS Publishing Company resources, visit our website at www.csspub.com, email us at csr@csspub.com, or call (800) 241-4056.

ISBN-13: 978-0-7880-2714-7
ISBN-10: 0-7880-2714-X

PRINTED IN USA

Table of Contents

Introduction

Over forty years ago, CSS Publishing Company was founded by two pastors and a Sunday school superintendent who had a vision to assist pastors "on the front lines" in their efforts to share the gospel of Jesus with people over the entire United States. The lectionary was taking hold over the country in an effort to bring a common message to people, no matter where they worshiped.

Over the years, CSS has published many different products. Of the more than 1,700 publications that have been produced in the history of the company, **Emphasis: A Lectionary Preaching Journal** has been one of the most popular. In its history, thousands of pastors and their congregations have benefited from the commentaries and insights found within its pages.

Navigating the Sermon is a collection of commentaries from "Charting the Course," which is at the core of what **Emphasis** is about. For each Sunday in the Cycle C lectionary, the writers who contributed to these columns have provided thematic guidance drawing together the lessons for each Sunday in the church year. Not only have they provided one idea for each Sunday, but most days have multiple themes from which to choose.

We are excited to offer this new resource to the readers of **Emphasis**, both old and new, and pray that this book will be a blessing to you and an invaluable aid to your preaching ministry.

The editors of CSS Publishing Company

Ash Wednesday
Joel 2:1-2, 12-17
2 Corinthians 5:20b—6:10
Matthew 6:1-6, 16-21
Wayne Brouwer

Love that hurts

The story is told of a young girl whose very best friend lived just down the street. They were playmates and almost sisters, with visits back and forth nearly every day.

When Jennifer was killed in an automobile accident, Tracie and her family were drawn through the same trench of grief. Two families were heartbroken and shared the awful blackness of funeral clothing together.

The day after the funeral, Tracie disappeared for a few hours. Her mother was worried and searched the house and yard in growing concern. When she went out to the street in front of their home she saw Tracie at a distance, slowly meandering toward her on the sidewalk, oblivious to her surroundings.

"Where were you, Tracie?" her mom asked as she strode toward the young girl. "I was worried about you."

"I was at Jennifer's place," Tracie replied. "I was helping her mom."

"What were you helping her with?"

"Well, neither of us felt like doing much, so I just crawled up into her lap and helped her cry."

Sometimes we all need to cry, and now and again we need help to do it. In the passages for today, on this Ash Wednesday, tears and repentance, sorrow, and prayer and fasting and pain are the order of the day. Joel helps ancient Israel cope with a devastating famine that hints as a harbinger to God's greater judgments. Paul reminds the Corinthian congregation of his pain on their behalf, hoping to move them to tears of repentance. And Jesus simply assumes that we will give, pray, and fast, for in these disciplines our hearts become more fully aligned with the values of the kingdom of heaven.

Joel 2:1-2, 12-17

It was a plague of locusts that set the context for Joel's prophecy of judgment day. While farmers watched their crops sliced away by the unstoppable insect horde, cultural uneasiness set in and the prophet linked this disaster to God's ultimate punishment on sin. No illustrated message has ever been more graphic.

It has been repeated 1,000 times. One college professor presented his class syllabus on the first day of the new semester. He pointed out that there were three papers to be written during the term, and he showed on which days those assignments had to be handed in. He said that these dates were firmly fixed and that no student should presume that the deadline did not apply to her or him. He asked if the students were clear about this, and all heads nodded.

When the first deadline arrived, all but one student turned in their papers. The one student went to the professor's office and pleaded for more time — just a single day! The student spoke of illness and hardships that had prevented him from completing the assignment, but all the research was finished, and a few more hours would allow the paper to be ready. The professor relented and granted a one-day extension without penalty. The student was extremely grateful and sent a note thanking the professor profusely.

When the second deadline arrived, three papers were missing from the pile of student productions. The student who had previously asked for an extension was back, and so were two others. As before, all the reasons expressed for failure to complete the assignment were touching and moving and tear-jerking, and the professor again allowed some latitude. The deadline was set aside, and the papers were required by the end of the week. A veritable chorus of praise filled the professor's small office, and blessings were heaped upon him.

When the third due date arrived, the professor was inundated with requests for extensions. Nearly a quarter of the class begged for more time — many other assignments and tests were due, many books still needed to be read, much work was required this late in the semester. But this time the professor held firm. No extensions were to be given. Grades would be marked lower for tardiness. Stunned silence filled the classroom.

The large delegation that met the professor in the hallway near his office was very vocal in their anger. "You can't do this to us! It isn't fair!"

"What isn't fair?" asked the professor. "At the beginning of the term you knew the due date of each paper and you agreed to turn in your work at those times."

"But you let so-and-so have extensions. You can't tell us now that we can't have a few extra days."

"Maybe you are right," said the professor. He opened his grade book and made a rather public subtraction from the grades given to the four formerly late papers. Each of those students, now also in this group, protested loudly. "You can't do that, professor! That's not fair!"

"What's not fair?" asked the professor. "Justice or mercy?" The question blanketed them heavily as each student silently slipped away. And the professor? When he reported the incident to others, he simply concluded (paraphrasing Henry Higgins from *My Fair Lady*), "They'd grown accustomed to my grace!"

We grow easily accustomed to God's grace. We need to become "Wow!"ed again by the amazing thing that happens when God chooses to start over in love toward us, even after the "great syllabus" demands a divine reckoning. No partnership can stretch forever to cover bad behavior or infidelity. Judgment day invariably comes.

Yet the prophecy of Joel carries with it more than warnings of God's grim reaping. In the divine matrix, justice is always wedded to mercy. The prophet, therefore, includes a call to a day of fasting, a solemn assembly in which hearts are turned and consciences cleansed before the Holy One. While the actual response of the people in Joel's day is unknown, the prophet ends his short messages with scenes of refuge and pledges of a world renewed. This is not only a theological promise for the future of humankind; it is also the hope we cling to when our relationships wander through rough places. God will guard the hearts that trust him even in the difficult times. Those who hear the warnings of a prophet like Joel can also be surprised by the miracle of a lover's care.

2 Corinthians 5:20b—6:10

Second Corinthians is actually the fourth of Paul's letters that we know about posted from Ephesus to the Peloponnesian Peninsula in the middle years of the 50s AD. Paul had stationed himself for three years in Asia Minor, working from Ephesus as a base of operations. But Corinth, the city that was his home for the bulk of his second mission journey, was much on his mind. Early in Paul's time at Ephesus, he heard news of gross immorality afflicting the congregation he loved deeply and sent a harsh letter of reproof.

The response was underwhelming. Some in Corinth held up his scathing indictment as the letter of the law, but many questioned and challenged Paul's right to meddle in their affairs now that he was no longer a pastor-in-residence. Divisions and jockeying parties sprang up in the church until it looked like the United Nations on summer recess.

Those still in leadership positions were worried. They decided to send a letter and a delegation to Paul, hoping that a personal visit would take the edge off Paul's passionate anger, and a few theological questions would turn everyone's attention away from the ethical and moral morasses in which they were stuck. In fact, it seemed to make a difference. The outcome was another letter from Paul, but this one more focused on the big picture issues of church development. It enters our New Testament as 1 Corinthians.

The success of that encounter seemed to give Paul reason to believe he had regained a place of authority in speaking to the problems of the Corinthian congregation. Therefore, he wrote another letter and sent it under the personal care of Titus. This epistle, however, was evidently vitriolic, for Paul himself acknowledged that it caused the congregation great sorrow and deeply hurt them (2 Corinthians 7:8). His words here in 2 Corinthians 5-6 are an attempt to explain more carefully that what he hoped would happen is a show of repentance among the Christ-believers in Corinth and a renewal through reconciliation.

Paul's litany of hardships is designed to show the depth of commitment he has for the Corinthian congregation. If he were not so deeply tied to them in love he would not care so ponderously for their welfare. It is like the parent who tells the child before a punishment, "This hurts me more than it hurts you." No child believes it, of course. Not until that child has grown and brought other children into this world. Then, suddenly, the full awareness of parental care floods home, and the tears of a child gush fountains from the eyes of a father. Paul hopes that something of this testimony of love will be reciprocal, and that those who write him off too quickly as a lame-duck departed authoritarian fool will peer into his heart and know that his call to repentance and renewal is rooted in the twin bonds that bind God and Paul to this rascally but revered church.

Matthew 6:1-6, 16-21

The Sermon on the Mount is the longest teaching of Jesus recorded in the gospels. By way of a number of clues, Matthew gives clear indication that he wants us to see Jesus as the new Moses, bringing the deepened word of God to a new age of the kingdom. Jesus goes up the mountain (5:1) as did Moses, and the major elements of the original covenant document in Exodus 20-24 are restated and then deepened and broadened in impact. Even at the close of the sermon in chapter 7, Matthew tells us that people marveled at Jesus' teachings, finding them more authoritative than those of the scribes. The implication is clear: The scribes only interpret the teachings of Moses, but Jesus brings a new word like Moses.

In the verses for today, Jesus addresses public acts of kingdom living — almsgiving, prayer, and fasting. It is interesting to note, first of all, that Jesus expects these practices to be part of the lifestyle of those who are his disciples and citizens of the kingdom of heaven. These are not optional activities but essential behaviors. To be a follower of the ways of the God of the covenant is to care for the poor, to pray, and to fast.

Almsgiving requires at least three stages of investment. The first is awareness. One cannot give alms without having the eyes to see where the need is and who personifies that impoverishment. This is illustrated by a fascinating incident from early in the church's history. According to Edward Gibbons, in his masterful treatise, *The Decline and Fall of the Roman Empire*, Antonius Pius, who ruled from 138-161 AD, was one of the best of Rome's rulers. During his days there was more wealth, business success, and domestic peace than most civilizations have known.

Antonius Pious was a good ruler, and his people knew it. In fact, one of his biggest supporters was the Athenian philosopher Aristedes, who lauded the emperor on many occasions. One day, however, Aristedes sent Antonius Pious a letter in which he urged the ruler to observe and imitate a particular group of people in the kingdom. "In all your grand empire they are the only ones who make it a habit to see the needs of the poor and do something about it," wrote Aristedes. Who was he referring to? Christians — disciples of Jesus who had learned to see.

A second dimension of almsgiving is the actual sharing of substance. Fiorello La Guardia was a police court judge before he became mayor of New York during the Great Depression. One cold winter's night, a man was brought to him charged with stealing a loaf of bread. The man acknowledged his guilt, noting that it was the only way he could provide food for his family. La Guardia pronounced judgment and fined the man $10, knowing that the thief could not possibly pay up.

Instead of sending the guilty party to jail, La Guardia pulled $10 out of his own wallet to pay the fine. Then he took back the $10, suspended the sentence, and fined everyone in the courtroom 50¢ for living in a city where a man has to steal bread in order to eat. When the man left the courtroom that day he had light in his eyes and $47.50 in his pocket.

Thirdly, almsgiving involves compassion, the quality of sharing in the plight of another with more than flippant handouts. Said Ralph Waldo Emerson, "Rings and jewels are not gifts, but apologies for gifts. The only gift is a portion of thyself."

Jesus' words about prayer remind us to ask ourselves why we want to pray in the first place. Bill Keane, in one of his delightful *Family Circus* comic strips, once showed little Jeffy picking up his football and looking forlorn because it was flat. A car had run over it. Little Jeffy says to himself, "I need a new football. I don't know if I should send up a prayer, write a letter to Santa Claus, or call Grandma." We may laugh at his dilemma, but it digs deeper into most of our psyches than we would care to admit. Jesus uses the illustration of some who treat prayer as simply another form of getting things we want, whether goods or esteem, even in a religious community. Do we seek the honor or approval of others or is there a ready relationship that is in place with God?

Prayer, according to Jesus, means that we recognize our truest needs and also recognize the one who cares for us more than we can even care for ourselves. One writer tells of a kindergarten class that took a field trip to a fire station. A firefighter told the children what to do in case of fire. "First you go to the door," he said, "and you feel it to see if it's hot. Then you get down on your knees. Does anyone here know why you do that?"

"Sure," said one of the little ones. "You get down on your knees to ask God to get you out of this mess." While not all prayers are made in the heat of fiery conflagrations, there is a refreshing honesty about that child's understanding of prayer.

When Jesus continues and addresses the concept of fasting, he again assumes this practice will permeate the community of his disciples. While we may think of fasting as culturally conditioned and best left in the world of first-century Judaism, it would be well to give it another consideration. In biblical times, people fasted for three specific reasons. The first was repentance: David fasted after he was caught in his sin with Bathsheba; the people of Nineveh fasted when Jonah shouted the impending judgment of God; the Israelites fasted every day of atonement, and many times in between. Second, fasting was a way of remembering: when King Saul and Prince Jonathan died in battle with the Philistines, David called the nation to fast and remember; Daniel fasted when he recalled the destruction of Jerusalem; and in Jesus' day there was an annual fast to remember the holocaust that nearly wiped out the Hebrew race when the hordes of Babylon swept down from the hills of Ephraim. Third, fasting was a way in which people could rivet their attention on God, keeping the body uncomfortable while the mind was clarified. Jesus himself expressed this fasting activity during his forty-day wilderness preparation for ministry. He was only following in the fine footsteps of Queen Esther who readied herself for an encounter with King Xerxes by fasting, and Ezra who joined fasting and prayer as his final act of readying the returning exiles before they took to the wilderness road between Babylon and the ruins of Jerusalem.

Fasting is not dieting. It is, instead, a declaration of the religious truth that we are not mere consumers who live for our bellies. Furthermore, it is a way of saying, "No," so that we can determine where, in fact, we will say, "Yes," and mean it truthfully out of our relationship with God. Those who cannot say, "No," do not know what it means to say, "Yes."

Application

On this Ash Wednesday, there is no greater application than to point people's eyes to the suffering Savior. We begin today the forty-day walk to the cross, sensing anew the growing heaviness in Jesus' heart, the weariness of his shoulders as the burden of the world collapses upon them, the aching of his spirit in the knowledge of what looms ahead, and the resolute resignation of his voice as he speaks increasingly about what will be done to him when he arrives in Jerusalem.

If we keep one eye and ear on Jesus, and then observe Joel and Paul with the other eye and ear, we will have a good stereo effect to elicit the proper pain of those who have a deeply symbiotic spiritual kinship with their Savior.

An Alternative Application

Matthew 6:1-6, 16-21. It might be possible to abstract the verses on fasting from Jesus' words in the Sermon on the Mount and use them as a model for today's demeanor. There is a poem by Edna St. Vincent Millay that brings us into the mood of fasting as we enter our own fasts during this Lenten season:

> *I drank at every vine.*
> *The last was like the first.*
> *I came upon no wine*
> *So wonderful as thirst.*
> *I gnawed at every root,*
> *I ate of every plant.*
> *I came upon no fruit*
> *So wonderful as want.*
> *Feed the grape and the bean*
> *To the vintner and the monger;*
> *I will lie down lean*
> *With my thirst and my hunger.*

Getting started on the right foot

We now set sail for Jerusalem, the events of holy week, and the hope of Easter morning. There is the old New England story of the farmer that, in giving driving instructions to the flatlander, informs the person that they can't get there from here. The story's humor revolves around the absurdity of such a statement. Of course you *can* get there from here. However, as I have watched the changing of the guard on Parliament Hill in Ottawa, Canada, I have noticed that before they actually begin there has to be a lot of shuffling and rearranging of ranks. In their case, if they do not start off on the right foot from the right place, they will not wind up where they need to be. Lent is more like the changing of the guard than like the story of the New England farmer.

Each of these texts helps us to identify where we begin our Lenten journey. They help us begin at the right place so that we can come out at a good place and be ready for the good news of Easter.

The text from Deuteronomy gives us our Jewish roots as the starting point for our journey. It is a good place to begin. Often, the Lenten journey has wound up in the bad place of anti-Semitic charges of Christ killer and hideous readings of scripture that imply the events of Holy Week will not only leave Judaism behind but will leave many Christians with a false sense of superiority regarding the Hebrew's story. If this is where we end up, then we certainly have gotten off to a bad start.

The lesson from Deuteronomy reminds us that we cannot get a grasp of what God is setting before us without coming to terms with what the journey has meant up to now. If this is what God has been up to in leading us in the past, then the journey ahead is about more than individual salvation or personal immortality.

The letter to the Romans proclaims that everyone who calls on the name of the Lord shall be saved. As part of the journey, it invites us to consider having our destinies tied to people of different customs and habits. Though the Lord may not make distinctions, we certainly do. If the starting point is that Jesus is Lord, then we are in for quite a journey. The Gentiles are a pretty broad and diverse category of people. If we begin with the lordship of Jesus, the engrafting of people can lead in many directions. However, if we do not begin with this lordship of Jesus, then we may not arrive at the place God intends for us.

The gospel lesson tells the tale of how Jesus' journey began following his baptism. You hardly catch your breath and Jesus barely comes up out of the water when he is plunged into the desert: tempted by the devil, hungry, and on his own. Can you get there from here? The truth is that we often wind up in the wrong place because we have not started with our real hungers and we have often wrongly tried to satisfy them. We often wind up out of step with each other because the steps that we have taken to get power, security, and prosperity are taking us seriously off target on our journeys.

Each of these texts raises the issues of where is the beginning point in my journey and with whom do I share the journey? I believe if these questions are our starting point in the Lenten pilgrimage, then we have an opening to where God wants us to land.

Deuteronomy 26:1-11

The text suggests that our starting point in the journey is "the land that the Lord your God has given you." My traditional faith upbringing tells me the starting point of Lent is my personal sins and what I have given myself over to that is blocking my relationship with God. This text seems to be quite a broad and expansive concept to be part of our Lenten luggage. However, the starting point in arriving at the place God wants us to be is the realization that land has been given as a gift. The starting point is asking, "Has the gift generated appreciation, gratitude, and sharing a sense of abundance?" The starting point may be that land rather than being treated as a gift, becomes something to be fought over. We have been given a place but many are homeless. We do not feel at home because more than 30,000 square feet of living space is needed. We have land issues.

The text makes clear that we were plucked from obscurity by this gift of land. By God's action, we have become a people with a history. Once we were only singular, a wandering Aramean, but by God's action we have become communal with dreams to share and visions to work out and a story to live out. But something happened in Egypt that happens to all who become communal. We become national as well as communal. As part of that system, as run by the Egyptians, we become enslaved to brick making. Education becomes about the number of credit hours you need and the letter grade you get. Medicine becomes mountains of paperwork and number of patients seen. Security becomes more about how high walls can be built rather than how contacts across borders can be made.

More and more bricks are on order to build the edifices of empires but the love of learning takes a backseat. The first brick is put into place by admission to the right preschool that will enable you to matriculate at the right private school and so advance to Skull and Bones at Yale or its equivalent. Healing begins to be second fiddle to cost effectiveness. Taking care of business becomes more important than taking care of yourself or of souls as we work longer hours and give up more vacation time.

That can happen to you in Egypt. By its very nature that is what Egypt and Egyptian thinking can do to you. The next thing you know you are enslaved to the notion that life cannot be good without that 30,000-square-foot house — more bricks. The only reward, as the Hebrews found out, for being able to make more bricks is the demand that you make more bricks. This is what has happened and does happen to us when we live in Egypt.

The story is not all about us. "The Lord, the God of our ancestors, the Lord heard our voice and saw our afflictions." It does not say that this voice was one of prayer. It is not a voice that has gotten its theological i's dotted and t's crossed. It is not a voice that is even directed to God or one that speaks with only one accent. Yet, God hears this voice. At the starting of a Lenten journey, I realize my need to repent for not speaking in this voice. We often try to fancy up our situation with theological language that we think will capture God's attention. The good news is that we already have God's attentiveness; we need only speak in a voice that reflects our genuine anguish.

What is also good news is that God will act on what God sees and hears. This is our story as well. There have been signs and wonders: walls do come crashing down, apartheid and segregation end, empires do not hold on forever. This is good news for the poor, but unfortunate for those who have gone down to Egypt to make their fame and fortune, and for all who are good and tired of making bricks. It is very bad news for those who are building their towers like Babylon or requisitioning more bricks for walls.

Romans 10:8b-13

Confessing that "Jesus is Lord" is one of the hardest things to do as I consider the starting place of my Lenten journey. As I consider Calvin's understanding of Jesus in his *Institutes of Religion*, I find it much easier to confess Jesus as prophet or priest than king. I feel comfortable with the first two roles no doubt because they spring directly out of specific religious connotation. I can see myself in the role of prophet speaking truth to power. I can understand one of the fundamental roles of ministry as priests mediating the presence of God through the rites and rituals of the church. That is as far as it gets. I have real trouble with identifying with the lordly virtues of kingship. I look at the assortment of modern possibilities for naming Jesus and the ones who come to mind feel pretty comfortable: wisdom teacher, therapist, visionary, marginal Jew, and so on. They all have their appeal. However, when it comes to what Paul writes to the Romans, I can feel the mental and spiritual brakes screeching as my faith understanding heads for a derailment.

It is a role that I am uncomfortable giving to Jesus and one that I am uncomfortable taking in ministry. I like Jesus as friend, I like to be friendly. I like Jesus as helper; I like to be thought of as helpful. I like to think of myself as a prophet of justice and I like seeing Jesus in the same way. I even graduated from a seminary, Lancaster Theological Seminary, that had the nickname "The School of the Prophets." It never occurred to anyone that the nickname "School of the Lords" would be appropriate.

Perhaps, however, the starting point for my Lenten journey is the realization that I need to pay attention to what Paul is saying here. Certainly in the Roman world, saying that Jesus is Lord is quite a claim. In our world, making this claim is no less vital. It is not just a claim that challenges Roman gods, it also challenges a world where many would make a god of the free market or anything else that would satisfy human wants.

Theologically, I am comfortable with the Jesus who says that he "stands at the door and knocks" and if anyone would let him come in, he would dine with them. However, I am less sanguine about the Jesus who ignores locked doors, who comes and barges right in and stands in the midst of the disciples after Easter morning. The Jesus who cannot be barred in the exercise of his lordship is, I suspect, somewhat threatening. The Jesus watching and waiting until we are ready is appealing to most. There is hardly a church that could not find in its church building somewhere an artistic representation of these words from the book of Revelation. However, it seems somewhat harder to find any painting or sculpture of the Jesus who comes into the midst of the disciples despite their attempts to wall out the external world.

I, too, wonder if my discomfort with this role for Jesus is really my discomfort with this role in ministry. Where does authority arise and how should it be exercised? Do other factors pretending to lordship creep into our lives so that we find ourselves serving false masters? One wonders what would have happened to the sex scandals among clergy if the churches had responded, "No one who believes in him will be put to shame."

Paul says it is not adequate to make the statement, "Jesus is Lord" only in one's heart. Putting it on your lips has a way of making it real in a way that keeping it inside does not. Putting it on the lips makes it a matter of conversation. No one should offer obedience without some conversation with those who find the concept of kingship and lordship difficult and offensive in their experience. The starting point of my Lenten pilgrimage is in part repentance for not having been more of a part of that conversation.

Luke 4:1-13

He is in the wilderness or the uninhabited place. It is usually in such places that these temptations come at us. However, the kind of temptation that Jesus struggles with seems alien to us. Does it really boil down to this way or that way? In making our life choices, we usually need to balance one interest after another. Can we see where the devil is coming from in this case? Is there not a case to be made here on his behalf? After all, if we could turn the world's stones into bread, we could make quite a dent in world hunger. Is there not a place, despite all the moral compromises involved, for taking charge with authority and power in the world? Is not one of the chief complaints against the peacekeeping capabilities of the United Nations that the UN is nothing but a well-intentioned, weak ineffectual presence in the world? One can certainly make out the case for Jesus being protected from certain death at least for what turned out to be his short life. Wouldn't it have been wonderful if Jesus had been around long enough to keep on as teacher and offering all those wonderful stories? If he had been protected from death if only for a bit longer would we not have had some answers for all those thorny questions that can get raised in confirmation classes? Would it have hurt for just a few more miracles to become the occasion for the miracle of more people coming to faith? There is a case to be made for the devil here.

The problem here is that no matter how eloquently the case can be made, it cannot be squared with the Spirit that has filled Jesus' soul, the scripture that falls from Jesus' lips, or the worship that Jesus' Spirit offers. When I yield to temptation and find myself off course from where God wants me to be, it is the result of failing to make these things the center of my being. Having made most of the headway in my life through using my brain, I am only more than ready to listen to well-reasoned arguments even if they come from the devil. Indeed only when I find myself beginning to listen to devilish arguments do I realize how I have wandered from what ought to be the starting point of my life.

Of course, wouldn't it be wonderful if we could turn stones into bread. However, the problem in the world is not that we do not have an adequate supply of bread. The problem is that we do not have a distribution system that faithfully shares the abundance we do have. The devil has conveniently left this out of the equation. Shall Jesus turn just enough stones into bread to satisfy his own needs? Such basic selfishness seems part of the world's problems right now. Shall he make enough bread from stones to satisfy the world's problems while leaving the distribution network to the devil? That, too, seems to be part of the world's problems as too many have too little, too few have too much, and the price on the wrapper that goes around the bread is more than the farmer gets for the wheat that goes into the bread. If your soul is set on the Holy Spirit, if a knowledge of scripture is at your fingertips, and you engage in holy worship, you tend to pick up on these things.

Of course, all the kingdoms come at a price. All you need to do is to stop worship as we know it and everything will be fine. All you need to do is to no longer make daily bread the aim; stop praying, "thy kingdom come." Make sure those who trespass somehow into your territory know about it in no uncertain terms before you even think of owning up to the number of times you have trespassed against them. Would any of the kingdoms of the world be worth very much if we lived in a world like that? People who are up on their scripture know these things; people who walk in the Spirit see through this offer.

The final temptation offers thoroughgoing protection from all of the exposure that the rest of the world has. Of course, thoroughgoing protection will result in complete disconnection from the reality of life as the rest of us experience it. Who would want to go and worship at that altar? It is tempting to be super human but the promises of God come to a head in the one who is fully human — Jesus the Christ.

People who are filled with the Spirit, have the words of scripture at hand, and who know what right worship is pick up on these things as the starting points for their lives.

Application

Saint Paul wrote that we should run the race that is set before us. A good part of the battle is getting to the starting line. A few years ago, when I ran my first 10k race, I learned what that meant. In the race that is set before us, there are no shortcuts and no getting there without getting to the starting line first. This would seem rather obvious until you realize at Lent how easy it is to wander off the course from the start.

My faith journey is rooted in the sad story of a people who are called out and made a community by the gift of God. Yet, they cave into the temptation of living the "Egyptian" lifestyle. My faith journey begins with the knowledge that God hears their complaints and our complaints when that happens. In my reluctance to give Jesus lordship as much a starting place as his friendship, I wonder how far off course I have become. No doubt about it, reason should be one of the supports of faith, and a faith that defies too much reason can be off the mark. Yet, I wonder how vulnerable I am to temptation when reason — more than right worship, more than the right relationship to the Holy Spirit, and more than the righteousness of God made known in scripture — is my first line of defense.

Lent invites us to ponder these questions in order that we may find ourselves on course for the good news of Easter.

An Alternative Application

Romans 10:8b-13. All my life I have seen signs that say, "Jesus saves." What is behind the signs means many things to many people. There seems to be near unanimity in agreeing with Paul that everyone who calls on the name of the Lord shall be saved — whatever that may mean. I must admit that I come from a tradition that has some skepticism in regard to that language. Putting a sign on the front lawn of our church to the effect that "Jesus saves" would get the phones in our congregation and community buzzing.

We have in the lectionary texts the recitation of great saving moments in the history of the Hebrews, which they owned and celebrated. It might be quite a sermon to celebrate just what have been those times in the life of your congregation when you felt that the "Lord had heard your voice and saw your affliction and acted to free you from bondage." It might make quite a beginning to Lent to gather in stories from church members as to when they have felt such times in their lives and share that testimony with the entire congregation.

It seems particularly true in the kind of New England mainline Protestant church I serve that we need to repent of not telling and sharing these stories. We are particularly vulnerable to devilish temptations when we do not have a narrative that tells our history of salvation experiences.

Lent 2
Genesis 15:1-12, 17-18
Philippians 3:17—4:1
Luke 13:31-35
David Kalas

God of the ages

What is the relationship between the past, the present, and the future? What impact does one have upon the others?

Gamblers carefully review and evaluate the minutiae of a team's past performances in order to wager intelligently on their upcoming game. Investors track the trends in markets and sectors in order to guess what lies ahead for a given company, stock, or fund. And psychologists help troubled souls identify what events and influences in their past continue to impact them in the present.

Just as we ponder the effect of the past on the present and the future, we also discover that the future reaches back to influence the present. The routine business of preparing — whether for school, for an interview, for a trip, for work, or for retirement — demonstrates the impact that the future has on present priorities and decisions.

When we delve into the pages of scripture, however, we are introduced to a whole new understanding of the interrelationship between past, present, and future. Past is not as determinative as we human beings are naturally inclined to think. Instead, we discover that it is the far future that is meant to have the greatest impact on our present.

Genesis 15:1-12, 17-18

One of the great disservices that has been done to so many of the people in our pews is the association of the word "unquestioning" with the word "faith." In some teaching and preaching, the marriage has been explicit. And in many struggling, individual hearts, the connection is simply assumed. *To question is to doubt, and to doubt is to lack faith. Faith, therefore, must never question.* So goes the guilt-ridden logic.

Here in this passage, however, we have the great hero of faith, Abraham, and in one of his most notable moments of faith (see Romans 4). Yet Abraham speaks only three sentences in this episode and two of them are questions.

Many of your people and mine have been led to believe that faith and questions cannot go together, so they may also feel that reverence and candor are mutually exclusive in prayer. A generation or two that is accustomed to dressing up for church may also be in the habit of dressing up for God. They reserve for prayer a formality of language and a kind of filtered content that is directly the opposite of their other most familiar and intimate relationships. The candor of the biblical saints, therefore, can be a lesson to many of the people in our pews.

Abraham, faced with all that the Lord had given him, presumed to point out what God had not given him. What long-term good would additional blessings from God be to Abraham if he had no real heir? And note that Abraham put the matter squarely on God. It was neither chance nor human incapacity that had kept Abraham and Sarah from having children, but rather it was the Lord who had "given me no off-spring."

How refreshing Abraham's approach is for many of us. How liberating to be reminded that pretense is not reverence. It is not an act of faith to be dishonest with God. Rather, Abraham had a complaint — or at least a concern — and he was candid with his Lord about it. Surely it is more faithful to be honest with

God. Surely it is more faithful to bring our needs and concerns to him than to grumble about them to ourselves or pretend they don't exist. What so often passes for reverence in our sometimes shallow praying is, in fact, more of an insult to God — an insult because we presume not to be honest with God and an insult because we are afraid to be.

The Lord did not upbraid Abraham for his candor or his questions. Rather, God responded with promises, reassurances, and details. And Abraham believed him.

Abraham believed the Lord and the Lord reckoned it to him as righteousness. Paul regarded this episode as the great Old Testament evidence of his doctrine of justification by faith. In addition to that fundamental matter of our salvation, it is an important episode for us to remember in the midst of our day-to-day circumstances, as well.

See how improbable Abraham's belief was. Our natural tendency is to extrapolate from past trends in order to predict future developments. Because the line on the graph has gone down in each of the preceding eleven months, we expect it to go down further in the twelfth month. That extrapolation is where Abraham began — the concern that Eliezer would be his only heir — but his faith was able to look beyond that. If he had merely extrapolated — only reasoned and reckoned by his own understanding without the benefit of faith — then his calculations would have come up childless. But he believed God. Against all odds, he believed God.

God's essential promise to Abraham was that he would have many descendants who would possess the land. At the time God made that promise, however, Abraham had no natural descendants, no realistic possibility of having any, and the only piece of that land he would legally possess by the time of his death was a field that he purchased for the purpose of a burial ground (Genesis 23). The circumstances were not very promising. The Lord, however, was very promising. And Abraham believed the Lord.

Philippians 3:17—4:1

Television commercials and programs that feature dangerous activities are sometimes accompanied by the warning, "Do not try this at home." This kind of driving is fine for the professional stunt drivers on the closed course, but don't get any ideas. Don't try doing what they do.

Then, in contrast, see the apostle Paul. He is sitting in chains in a foreign prison, possibly facing execution. And from that location, Paul encourages the Philippian Christians, "Join in imitating me."

The man who discovers that he has walked into a minefield doesn't usually call out to those he loves, "Follow in my footsteps!" But from prison Paul urges his brothers and sisters in Christ to follow his example.

This is no case of "misery loves company," however. Quite the contrary: joy loves company and Paul is full of joy. Paul's letter to the Philippians has rightly earned the nickname "the joyful epistle," for his tone and vocabulary are conspicuously joyful, especially given his circumstances. It is the joy of knowing Christ, and Paul had personally discovered that that joy eclipsed all of the attendant difficulties.

This excerpt from the joyful epistle is personal and poignant. Paul's deep love for the Philippians and his heartfelt emotion in writing to them is evident in the warmth and tenderness of his language. He refers to them twice as his "brothers and sisters." He tells them things "with tears." And the final verse of this passage (4:1) is so encumbered with expressions of love that it becomes awkward as a sentence.

The poignancy of the passage lies in the fact that Paul is writing from prison. The issue, though, is not that Paul feels sorry for himself in his present state. Rather, it is the poignancy of being separated from the Philippians. We all know that nothing is quite so frustrating to love as not being able to "be there." It is especially difficult when the ones we love are in the midst of some difficulty or danger.

Truthfully, Paul's own situation was far more difficult than the Philippians'. But the physical pain and peril he faced were not so compelling to Paul as the spiritual challenges facing the Philippians. The confinement and persecution Paul was experiencing did not seem to compare favorably to the self-indulgent hedonism he warns about (3:19) and yet he calls upon the Philippians to imitate him rather than those pleasure-seekers.

Set side by side, Paul's bread-and-water rations behind bars don't look so desirable as the all-you-can-eat-smorgasbord living of those who "live as enemies of the cross of Christ." On the other hand, if we set side by side the glory and beauty of Christ with "their god... the belly," if we set side by side a citizenship in heaven with the dust and disappointment of "earthly things," and if we set side by side "the body of his glory" with "the body of our humiliation," then suddenly there is no comparison. So Paul urges his beloved ones to imitate him and to "stand firm in the Lord."

Luke 13:31-35

It's always a bit suspicious when your opponents offer you advice. We see it routinely in the world of politics, as Democratic operatives give advice on television about what the Republicans should do, and vice versa. Likewise as the Pharisees come and offer ostensibly helpful advice to Jesus.

We don't have any evidence to confirm the report that Herod was eager to kill Jesus. On the contrary, he had long been too afraid to kill John the Baptist, with whom he had more of a personal complaint. After he finally arranged for John's execution, Herod was immediately haunted by the thought that Jesus was John come back to life (Matthew 14:2; Mark 6:16). Furthermore, when Jesus was brought to Herod in custody, Herod "was very glad, for he had been wanting to see him for a long time... hoping to see him perform some sign" (Luke 23:8). And given the opportunity to pass sentence on Jesus, Herod declined, returning Jesus to Pilate.

It seems much more likely, therefore, that the Pharisees were trying to make Jesus go away simply because they wanted him to go away. Just shortly before this episode, Luke reports that "the Pharisees began to be very hostile toward him" (Luke 11:53), and so it seems highly improbable that the Pharisees would try to protect Jesus from Herod.

Jesus was very shrewd about people's motives, and so he likely recognized that the Pharisees were not earnestly trying to protect him from Herod. His "go and tell that fox" statement, therefore, was probably meant as much for the Pharisees as for Herod.

Interestingly, the Pharisees were likely fabricating a death threat in order to scare Jesus away, he still went deliberately on his way toward Jerusalem, and he went precisely for the purpose of dying (see 13:33). In light of the cross and the empty tomb, how pathetic does the Pharisees' threat seem? Jesus had already eluded earlier efforts to kill him when the time was not right (Matthew 2:13-16; Luke 4:28-30; John 7:30, 8:59), and he made it clear even at the time of his arrest that he could be rescued simply by saying the word (Matthew 26:53). While the threat of death is the ultimate weapon the world can wield, it was an inadequate tool against Jesus.

Having expressed aloud his intent to go to Jerusalem to die, Jesus breaks into a lament about Jerusalem. The love-in-pain tone of Jesus' repeated vocatives ("Jerusalem, Jerusalem") might be best understood in light of other biblical examples of the same technique: "Simon, Simon" (Luke 22:31), "Martha, Martha" (Luke 10:41), "O my son Absalom, my son, my son Absalom" (2 Samuel 18:33), and "My God, my God" (Psalm 22:1; Mark 15:34). Facing the prospect of his own death, Jesus laments, but not for himself. Rather, he laments for Jerusalem, the city that not only declines the Lord's overtures but also violently rejects them. It may have been customary in some times and places to kill the messenger who brought bad news. What an irony, though, that Jerusalem chose again and again to kill the messengers who brought good news — loving exhortations and gracious salvation from God.

From the perspective of this side of the empty tomb, we understand better what Jesus said to Herod and to the disingenuous Pharisees. Jesus was not literally going to complete his work in the next 72 hours. Rather, he planted the cryptic seed of this lovely gospel truth that his work would indeed be finished "on the third day."

Application

The older we get, the more we come to recognize the interconnectedness of the past, the present, and the future.

We see the pendulum of fashion trends swing back and reintroduce styles that we remember from thirty years ago. We see how human relationships — whether between individuals, groups, or nations — are sweetened or embittered by the accumulation of past events. And we recognize more and more within ourselves the profound and continuing influence of our childhood experiences on our adult responses and behaviors.

At another level, when a medical doctor offers a patient a prognosis, it may come in the form of odds — say, a 40% chance of recovery. That prognosis for the future, however, is no more than a record of the past. Based on the past results of similar cases, we predict the future outcome of present cases.

At a personal level, you and I experience every day an assortment of common emotions — e.g., worry, hope, dread, regret, nostalgia, anticipation, and such — all of which bear witness to the enormous impact that past, present, and future have on one another.

The three lections we have before us this week also bear witness to the relationship of past, present, and future, but with a twist. The twist is faith. The twist is a recognition that we cannot really calculate the equation of past, present, and future without factoring in the God who is Lord of both time and eternity.

Abraham's past and present did not add up to the future that God had in mind. His past and present, so far as he could tell, added up to some slave from Damascus receiving all of his inheritance. But the sovereign God had a future in store where a whole nation of Abraham's descendants would inherit and settle the land where Abraham lived only as a sojourner. Descendants as many as Abraham could count would spread out over the land as far as Abraham could see. With God, Abraham's future was far more than a simple extrapolation of his past and his present.

Paul, meanwhile, urged the Philippian Christians to let their present be a kind of extrapolation of their future. Paul laid out for them an understanding of what the future held, on the one hand, for those who were "enemies of the cross of Christ" and, on the other hand, for those who were believers following his example. In the present, in a prison, Paul's approach did not look so good. But Paul looked to the future — God's future — and lived toward that.

Jesus predicted that his work would be finished on "the third day." Between that prediction and victory, however, came a lot of seeming troubles, setbacks, and defeats. We, in the midst of troubles, are likely to lose hope about the future. But, like Abraham and Paul, we serve a Lord who will indeed fulfill his promise and finish his work with victory.

Alternative Applications

Genesis 15:1-12, 17-18. Some of the big events in our lives are about plot. We get married, we have children, we move, we change jobs, we experience some loss or tragedy, we retire, and on it goes. The "plot" big events are often the kinds of occasions when we take pictures.

Other big events in our lives, however, are not about plot. They are about dialogue. They are instances when nothing visibly or measurably happens, but they are big events because of what is said.

At the opening of the scene in Genesis, Abraham has just come off of a series of big plot events. First, there was the ugly Egypt episode (12:10-20). Famine had forced a move by Abraham and Sarah, and then fear prompted them to be deceptive about their relationship. When the truth was discovered, they were summarily evicted from the land where they had sought refuge. Next came turmoil between his camp and the camp of his nephew, Lot, leading to their separation. Shortly after their separation, however, Lot's new home found itself in the crossfire of a regional conflict, and Abraham was forced to mobilize for a military rescue operation.

Life had not been peaceful and uneventful for old Abraham since leaving Ur. But then, "after these things," God came and spoke to Abraham. The next big event in Abraham's life was not about plot, it was about dialogue.

God spoke to Abraham. He spoke great promises. He spoke great improbabilities. "And he believed the Lord; and the Lord reckoned it to him as righteousness" (v. 6). It was an all-dialogue event, but it was seminal. Two thousand years later, the apostle Paul pointed to this event as not only pivotal for Abraham, but emblematic of the great pivotal event for all who are saved (see Romans 4 and Galatians 3).

The preacher and his/her people can embrace the truth of big events that are all dialogue. Precisely such events are sprinkled through our testimonies. Prayer itself is usually such an event. Anytime an occasion (like this Sunday morning) features a dialogue with God — his word to us and our faithful response to him — it is a big event.

Luke 13:31-35. From time to time in Bible study settings, I challenge people to make a list of the apparent shortcomings of God's people at the point in time being studied. For example, what were the recurring failures of the Israelites in the wilderness? What were the great sins cited by the eighth-century BC judgment prophets? What did Jesus need to correct and reprove among his disciples again and again? What were the concerns that prevailed in the local churches to which Paul wrote?

My contention is that we will seldom come across a shortcoming or sin that is unfamiliar to us. What we see in the pages of scripture, we are also very likely to see in the mirror. That is not to say that every individual is beset with the whole collage of human sinfulness. It is to say, however, that we don't usually have to look very far to see that the human condition and tendency is always pretty much the same.

Accordingly, it is worth considering at a personal level what Jesus says of Jerusalem. We may distance ourselves from this passage because we haven't stoned any prophets. The underlying issue, though, is how God's people respond to him and to his word.

We, perhaps more than any previous generation of God's people, are inclined to pick and choose what we like from God's word, biblical commands, and Jesus' teachings. We don't need to stone any prophets when we can simply reduce God's word to a smorgasbord for consumers.

Meanwhile, there is this God who seeks to gather his people, like a hen gathers her chicks under her wings. Do we come when he calls? Do we let God draw us near to himself? Or do we ignore his invitations, postpone our response, and resist a closer relationship and deeper discipleship?

Perhaps our own names should be inserted when we hear Jesus lament, "Jerusalem, Jerusalem!"

Lent 3
Isaiah 55:1-9
1 Corinthians 10:1-13
Luke 13:1-9
Timothy Cargal

Tumbling towers

I still remember that morning and I imagine that I will for the rest of my life. I was scheduled to have the first (and hopefully last) significant surgery of my life. I had arrived at the hospital very early that morning and had been taken back into the surgical preparation area. Initially everything was proceeding as scheduled but after a while everything just seemed to come to a halt. Oh, there was plenty of activity buzzing around, but the things I had been told would happen with me just weren't. I was growing impatient and irritated.

Then I began to pick up some buzz about a plane crash. It was hard to pull together details from what I was overhearing (no one was bringing me news directly, and there was no television where I was). It apparently had happened in New York. I could understand why everyone was talking about it, but I didn't see why it should have brought things to a halt in a suburban Washington hospital. Then the buzz seemed to be about a crash here in Washington. Was it a second crash or were they confused about where the crash had been in the first place? All that was clear was that I wasn't on anyone's agenda at the moment.

A short while later my surgeon arrived. All surgeries for that morning had been cancelled. Not one, but two planes had crashed into the World Trade Center Towers in New York, a third had crashed into the Pentagon little more than ten miles away, and a fourth plane was reportedly heading toward Washington. The operating rooms had been closed in order to deal with what was expected to be a flood of emergency cases.

The date, obviously, was September 11, 2001. For me, the events of that day were in some ways up close and personal but still primarily experienced through radio and television news reports. For the vast majority of Americans, that day was lived vicariously through the news media. The ability of millions to simultaneously share in an experience through mass media has created events that became defining moments in our culture. People can replay in intricate detail the circumstances that surrounded them and the emotions they felt when they first heard that news or that the Space Shuttle *Challenger* had exploded on lift-off, the *Columbia* had exploded during re-entry, Martin Luther King Jr., had been shot while standing on a balcony of a motel in Memphis, John F. Kennedy had been shot while riding in a presidential motorcade winding through the streets of Dallas, or Japanese warplanes had just destroyed much of the U.S. Pacific Fleet as it lay at anchor in Pearl Harbor.

Of all the national experiences that have been created by mass media, why is it these catastrophes stay with us so vividly and with such tenacity? It cannot just be their shock value or their overwhelmingly negative impact; we hear about many shocking evils every day. I am convinced that the impact of these events is that they serve as dramatic wake-up calls. Their significance in our minds goes far beyond the particulars of the individual events.

Not a few historians have concluded that the Civil Rights era begun in 1950s died as well on that Memphis balcony, for King's assassination and the rage of the riots that followed in its aftermath fundamentally changed once again the relationship among races in our country. Lee Harvey Oswald's bullet stole life not only from a young president but also from the idealism of America's "Camelot." The bombs dropped by Japanese Zeros not only set ablaze America's Pacific Fleet but left in ashes as well the nation's myth of geographic isolation bolstered and protected by unassailable military might. "9/11" did the same thing for a new generation. The very reason the first shuttle disaster is more etched on our memories than the second is because a whole worldview about the power and precision of technology, a mythology embodied for many by NASA, crumbled along with the *Challenger*, leaving room only for a "not again" reaction at the loss of *Columbia*. Such events lay waste to our carefully constructed worlds of human self-sufficiency.

Isaiah 55:1-9

Sometimes when you read the end of a book first you get a different sense of what it was about than if you had started at the beginning. Knowing how things will turn out and what will be important at the end of the day, as it were, focuses one's attention on different details at the beginning than might have been apparent without those clues. Reading from the end provides an interesting perspective on this particular scripture lesson.

The New Revised Standard Version provides the heading, "An Invitation to Abundant Life" for the oracle by the exilic prophet preserved in Isaiah 55. God's call to satisfy our thirst and hunger "without money and without price" in the opening verse certainly fits with the theme expressed by the heading. Yet the final verses of the reading emphasize lack rather than abundance, at least as regards human wisdom as compared to God's. The oracle insists that our thoughts and actions are as far removed from God's "as the heavens are higher than the earth" (v. 9). Now it could be argued that the prophet invites us to leave behind our lack for God's abundance, to "seek the Lord while God may be found" (v. 6), but one could also argue that the prophet is encouraging us to change our very notion of what counts as abundance.

Returning to the opening verses of the oracle, notice just how different are God's thoughts from the values that dominate our culture. God calls to those who "have no money, Come, buy and eat!" But what can it mean to "buy" if we give neither money nor bartered goods in exchange? To our "free market" world, God calls for everyone to come and receive the necessities of life for free. But we only assign value to things that have a price. Our slogan is, "You get what you pay for," and its corollary is that if you pay nothing then you get nothing of value. We want to be self-sufficient, to make our own way in the world; God calls us who thirst to come to the living waters by which God supplies life (v. 3).

What is God's assessment of the things that we do value? God simply asks each of us, "Why do you spend your money for that which is not bread, and your labor for that which does not satisfy?" (v. 2a). If we are so wise and self-sufficient, then why do we experience so much of life as lack rather than abundance? Our ideas of abundance always leave us hungering and thirsting for more. We need to "listen carefully" to God so that we will know what food is genuinely "good" and can bring "delight" to our lives. We need to elevate our thoughts by replacing our human values and wisdom with God's thoughts.

Such transformation of one's thinking lies at the heart of the biblical concept of repentance, and it is precisely the language of repentance that we find in the final verses of the reading (and the heart of the oracle as a whole). To "seek the Lord," "forsake" wicked ways, and "return to the Lord" (vv. 6-7) are all common expressions of repentance. As long as we think of life primarily in terms of things we can provide for ourselves, then we will be confused by the call to repentance of those who live in want. Those who do return to God and God's ways, however, will receive mercy and abundant pardon — truer marks of abundant life than any material goods one may amass no matter how necessary to physical life.

1 Corinthians 10:1-13

In this portion of his letter, Paul utilizes a classic form of argumentation that is usually referred to as either allegorical or typological. Almost every sentence of the reading bears an allusion to some event from the experience of the Israelites during the Exodus and subsequent period of wilderness wanderings. The specific source references for these allusions can be found in most any study, Bible or commentary, and so will not be repeated here. Paul himself refers to these allusions as "examples," and so we need to ask why he considers these the relevant or appropriate examples (vv. 6 and 11) for his Corinthian readers and what particular function does he hope these examples will play for his readers.

Regarding the initial part of our question, the simple answer as to why Paul chose these particular examples would seem to be that they parallel specific topics that he has already taken up in the letter. Concern with baptism (10:2; cf. 1:11-17), idolatry in the specific context of eating and drinking (10:7; cf. 8:1-13), sexual immorality (10:8; cf. 5:1-13), and complaints within the community and about its leadership (10:10; cf. 3:1-23; 6:1-11; 9:1-18) comprise the bulk of what Paul has written about to this point. Yet examples of all these things abound throughout the Old Testament. Might there be some further reason why Paul chose to cluster all his examples in the experience of Israel in the wilderness?

Perhaps there is one implicit parallel between the Israelites and the Corinthians that Paul wishes to draw out from his choice of these particular examples. Just as all the examples Paul offers are from the earliest period of Israel's communal experience as the people of God, the Corinthians are themselves flush with the experience of being a newly constituted community of God's people. Paul may have wished to suggest that there are particular dangers or risks that accompany a newly experienced awareness of God's grace and acceptance.

The conclusion that Paul draws from his typological argument would seem to support this view. "So if you think you are standing, watch out that you do not fall" (10:12). Those who realize they have been brought into covenant with God as a result of God's grace rather than their own worthiness may be tempted to libertarian excess. God chose us when we were sinners, so would God reject us now if we continue in our sin? But just as the biblical story of the Israelites shows that they put their participation in the covenant at risk by such behaviors, Paul now warns the Corinthians that they run the risk of following exactly the same course.

Beyond providing a warning, Paul also emphasizes "God is faithful" (10:13). The God who brought the Israelites and the Corinthians into covenant will also help keep them within that relationship. The experience of the Israelites and the Corinthians is "common to everyone," and God will intervene to limit the severity of the temptations and to assist in withstanding them. Although the Israelites were tempted to abandon their covenant with God, God would ultimately abandon them. The same would be true for the Corinthians and for us.

Luke 13:1-9

Jesus suggested that two catastrophic events contemporaneous to his own ministry destroyed any sense of self-sufficiency for those who had heard about them. His comments were prompted by a report that the Roman governor Pontius Pilate had ordered the massacre of a group of worshipers from Galilee, mixing their human blood with the blood of the sacrificed animals. The report here in Luke is the only record of this particular atrocity, but it is in keeping with what the contemporary Jewish historian Josephus reports about Pilate's actions against those under his authority (killing Samaritans on their way to worship at Mount Gerizim and diverting funds from the Jerusalem temple's treasury and desolating it with Roman images, provoking riots; *Antiquities* 18.55-62, 85-89).

Jesus related this political tragedy to another recent event where the culpability was hardly obvious. A tower had collapsed, killing eighteen people who were standing nearby. Now there was a widely held view among Jews at that time — a view still found among even some Christians to this day — that physical suffering, whether as a result of illness or disaster, was a direct consequence of sin and a clear indication of divine judgment. Jesus rejected such a simplistic notion outright. Were those who died at Pilate's hand or those crushed by the tower worse sinners than those who escaped with their lives? Jesus answers the question directly: "No, I tell you; but unless you repent, you will all perish just as they did" (v. 5).

If you listen carefully to what Jesus said, it would seem that he takes away with one hand what the other had just granted. No, Jesus insisted, those who died in these disasters were no worse than anyone else. You cannot draw conclusions about a person's morality from the tragedies that occur in their life. "But," Jesus continued, "unless you repent you will all perish just as they did." We are quick to object. "Now wait just a minute, Jesus! If repentance, asking God's forgiveness for our sins, can spare us from perishing as those did in these tragedies, aren't you saying that there *is* a connection between sin and suffering in a person's life?"

It was to head off just such an objection that Jesus immediately related the parable of the fig tree. Jesus wanted to make clear what was wrong with the old way of thinking. The problem was not with the notion of divine judgment. Just as the fig tree, if it failed to produce in response to the gardener's careful attention, would be cut down at the end of the next growing season, so was it true that there will be those who will ultimately suffer God's judgment. Their belief in divine judgment was not the problem; their problem was in their blithe assumption that their comfortable lives were proof they were already immune to such judgment.

The point of Jesus' assertion that the victims were not any worse than the survivors was not to rehabilitate the reputations of the dead but to challenge the living to see that they were no better than those who had been overcome by tragedy. It was not their superiority that had spared them, but God's grace in continuing to care for them, to nurture them like the gardener tending the fig tree. "There, but for God's grace, go I!" Jesus' point in relating the parable in response to the disastrous news that was buzzing about the people was that while they could see what was happening, they were not understanding it correctly (cf. Luke 12:54-56). Where we see divine punishment in the disasters, we should rather see a call to repentance. Where we see divine approval in the care given to the unproductive fig tree, we should actually see divine mercy. Even given God's grace, there are limits to the divine patience. The clock is ticking for the fig tree, and the clock is ticking for each of us.

Application

How are we to respond to this realization? Jesus said that in order to avoid "perish[ing] just as they did" we must repent. Repentance means much more, however, than simply acknowledging that we have done wrong and asking for God's forgiveness. Genuine repentance involves a change of our minds. It only really happens when our view of the world is changed, when we reject the notion of human self-sufficiency in favor of the truth of our dependence upon the divine.

Too often we have watered down repentance in our minds to something like this: "God, I know that you — for some reason — have a problem with this kind of behavior. Now, I don't pretend to understand why you get so upset about this, but I do know that I don't want you mad at me. So please forgive me this time, and I'll try not to do it again." That is not real repentance because that is being sorry that you got caught and being afraid to face the consequences. Real repentance comes when we begin to see the world the way God sees it, to understand the harms God's prohibitions direct us away from and the joys God's commands bring to our lives, to recognize God is not a cosmic killjoy but a loving and patient parent. That is why these events that shatter our preconceived notions about the world — whether towers fall on the unsuspecting, or vibrant, young leaders are felled by assassins' bullets, or technological marvels cataclysmically fail — provide occasions for genuine repentance.

Repentance arises not from fear of punishment but from realization with the prophet that God's wisdom is of an astronomically higher order than human wisdom. Indeed, as Isaiah reminds us, our vaunted wisdom leads to the foolishness of valuing what is ultimately worthless and of despising what has true value. Our problem is not just sins, the numerous ways in which we waste our "money," as it were, buying things that cannot satisfy us and only bring harm to others. Our problem is sin, the inability to recognize the lack of ultimate value in what we desire, the ability to deceive ourselves into thinking we are self-reliant when truly we are dependent upon God. Repentance is replacing human value judgments with divine ones.

Jesus does not call us either to blithely accept suffering as inevitable or to acquiesce to suffering as divine judgment. He calls on us to change ourselves through genuine repentance and to change the world by bearing the fruit of that repentance. They may not have the sudden and dramatic impact upon our emotions and psyches as disasters or assassinations, but in their own ways the disciplines of Lent are also about calling us to reconsider our view of the world. It is a time to ask ourselves if the values that truly govern our lives as we go about our daily business, are the same values that motivate God to action. Lent is a season of repentance, a time not only to seek forgiveness for our failures to God and others, but a time to "be transformed by the renewing of [our] minds, so that [we] may discern what is the will of God — what is good and acceptable and perfect" (Romans 12:2b).

An Alternative Application

1 Corinthians 10:1-13. If the Israelites were an example to the Corinthians of the dangers of an incipient libertinism as they began their communal life as God's people, then both the Israelites and the Corinthians are examples to modern Christians as they continue their Lenten journey. The purpose of Lent is not to raise questions or doubts about our salvation. That is ultimately in God's hands. Lent should remind us of our need to respond to God's grace with faithful lives even as it heightens our awareness of the activity of God's grace in our lives.

Paul's use of a typological argument here also provides good homiletical guidance for modern preachers. He does not so much look for discrete, isolated parallels as for a pattern within the scriptural narrative that is played out again and again in the spiritual lives of God's people. Being able to see that pattern within the Bible helps us to recognize it within our own lives as well. In this instance that pattern serves to underline that such experience is "common to everyone," and then just as God has helped others in the past, so God will give us the assistance we need as well.

Always wanting more

With Augustine we can affirm that pride is the fundamental sin and concupiscence is its fundamental fruit. Pride manifests itself in America as we glory in the overall dominance displayed by our athletes during any Olympic games. Our expectations were expanded as athletes excelled and reaped multiple medals for their efforts. Experienced athletes from prior Olympics return to defend their titles. Sportscasters talk just as much about it in anticipation as they did following the competition.

As a human race, we are always striving for more and are usually not satisfied unless we achieve it. Sometimes this striving for more leads to some dire circumstances, like using illegal drugs to enhance physical performance in order to outdo the competition. Our decisions have consequences, some of which cannot be recalled or redeemed. Is this the way it is in terms of our spiritual journey through life — striving for more, but always being left wanting something better? How does this affect our relationship with God? How does God respond to this in us?

Joshua 5:9-12

It is fascinating to note in the Bible how names carry such significance. So often they express the essence of an event or the character in a person and serve as a reminder of the judgments and mercies of God. Gilgal and Gibeath-haaraloth are such names that signify something more than just the mere utterance of the word that is haphazardly attached to a particular place.

Joshua had assumed the leadership of the people after Moses died. He led them into Canaan, crossing the Jordan River. This crossing was a mini-version of the Red Sea episode. There they fled out of Egypt; here they marched into the Promised Land. There the pharaoh was finally impressed; here the kings of the Amorites and the Canaanites were impressed (Joshua 5:1).

A situation developed that needed redress. During the wanderings in the wilderness after the Exodus, a whole generation had arisen who had not been circumcised. Those who had originally come out of Egypt had been circumcised with the sign of the promise. But, because of their disobedience in the wilderness, they were not allowed to enter into the Promised Land. However, the generation born in the wilderness would be allowed to inherit the promise. But, they had not been circumcised. Now was the time to take care of that, so they would bear on themselves the sign of the covenant between God and the people, a sign that was originally given to Abraham (Genesis 17).

To commemorate this event of mass circumcision, the place became known as Gibeath-haaraloth, "the hill of the foreskins." It is a rather graphic name — one that pictures in its utterance what was done at this place to keep in step with God as the people prepared to take possession of the land. It was, however, by the name Gilgal that the place would be called. The word Gilgal comes from the Hebrew word meaning "to roll." As God said to Joshua, "This day I have rolled away the reproach of Egypt from you." God had done a new thing. (Is this, perhaps, a foreshadowing of rolling away the stone of enslavement to death?) Now that the people were poised to inherit the land, they needed to be reminded of what God had done for them. Naming the encampment Gilgal would do just that. The name expressed the meaning of their new status. No longer were they slaves in Egypt. They were a free people, ready to shine among the nations of the world. The reproach of their experience in Egypt was past, rolled away. Newly circumcised, they were ready to march forward into a future God had prepared for them.

The land held that future. Whereas manna had been provided in the wilderness for their daily needs, it was provisional. Now, they needed to settle on the land and work it and from it produce their daily staples. The psalmist would express years later, "Blessed is everyone who fears the Lord, who walks in his ways! You shall eat the fruit of the labor of your hands; you shall be happy, and it shall be well with you" (Psalm 128:1-2).

What is worth noting in all of this is that God is judging his people and showing mercy on them at the same time. The circumcised were brought out of Egypt in a great act of deliverance. When they disobeyed God, they were judged and kept out of the Promised Land. Still, their children would enter to fulfill the promise. Circumcision would continue to be the sign of the covenant to which God would be faithful and the people would be called and recalled to be faithful. The new generation and the generations to come would experience the judgment and mercy of God in different ways as they lived on the creases of an unfolding history that would move the promises of God to greater fulfillment. The people would learn that God was serious about his purposes in the world and their role in bringing them about. The sign of the covenant would forever be before them (Gibeath-haaraloth) and they would roll forward from the place of their encampment (Gilgal), remembering the new chapter that was being written with a new generation.

2 Corinthians 5:16-21

"From now on..." Something has happened to cause Paul to see things very differently. What was it? "From a human point of view..." no longer works to grasp "the breadth and length and height and depth" (Ephesians 3:18) of anything. The psychology of change tells us that people will accept a new paradigm when they have had a *significant emotional experience*. What was this for Paul and the early Christians who were willing to put their lives on the line and behave differently "from now on..."?

The context to understand these words can be found in 1 Corinthians 15 and also the two verses (2 Corinthians 5:14-15) that precede this text for today. Essentially, it was the death and resurrection of Jesus that presented that *significant emotional experience* for Paul and the church, such that "we regard no one from a human point of view." The originator of a *new age* theology is Paul, who announces in his gospel that anyone who is in Christ is a *new creation*. Former things do not count the same way anymore. There is a new paradigm that has seized the imagination. That paradigm is the death and resurrection of Jesus, which announces what God has done and is now doing in the affairs of the world.

First, God has reconciled the world to himself. This has been done through the death and resurrection of Jesus. His "act of righteousness leads to acquittal and life for all men" (Romans 5:18). His obedience reforms and makes righteous those who have been disobedient, but now trust in the unfathomable deeds of God rather than their own doings. The gospel has superceded the law (Romans 3:20-26) as the foundation on which to stand righteous before God. The writer to the Hebrews (9:26b-28) and 1 John (4:10) express this in terms of atonement theology. In Jesus, a new order has been established in which God has revealed his heart for the salvation of the world, definitively creating a new relationship between heaven and earth — the cross of Christ being the new logo.

This opens the door to a new way of relating to one another on a human plane. Paul applies the reconciliation achieved between God and humanity to the purpose of his personal ministry as a follower of Christ. "All this is from God, who... gave us the ministry of reconciliation" (5:18). There has been great dissension in the Corinthian church. Paul has been writing to these folks (probably at least three times!) attempting to iron out the creases that have wrinkled their witness to the gospel. Reconciliation is needed in the church in Corinth. Paul describes himself as an ambassador for Christ, appealing to them on behalf of God to get their act together. Their disagreeableness with one another means that they are at odds with

God. As they live in the reconciliation offered by Christ, they will discover a new way to regard one another — no longer from a human point of view!

Paul understands himself as an ambassador for Christ, speaking on his behalf to those who would claim to be followers. Talk about career confidence! Going right to the heart of the matter — that what is at stake is not just one's relationship with brothers and sisters in Christ, but also with Christ himself — Paul beseeches (*doemai*; to entreat, pray; the earnestness of this word is also expressed in 8:4 and 10:2) his Christian friends to "be reconciled to God." That is to say, return to the only ground on which to stand, the ground of Calvary, where Christ worked out the saving reconciliation that makes us right with God! It is from this ground that we can venture forth in right step with one another, modeling ourselves the reconciliation that Christ continues to work in the world.

Luke 15:1-3, 11b-32

Ever since the wilderness wanderings, the people of God have had a fondness for murmuring. There was no exception in Jesus' day. The religious elite, namely the Pharisees and scribes, had a rather snooty attitude toward the more unseemly characters of society. When the tax collectors and sinners were attracted to Jesus so that they might hear him, these religious snobs took notice and immediately criticized Jesus' choice of company. Contrasting these two social groups, one can hear even more the biting irony of Jesus' words, "Whoever has ears to hear, let them hear!"

'Amartwlov, which is related to *amartia* — the most frequently used word for sin in the New Testament as well as the Septuagint, designates one who has failed to live up to a standard, whether by action or inaction, intentional or unintentional. The tax collectors, thieves, and prostitutes were numbered among those. If one wished prestige in the community, it would be a social gaff to be associated with the likes of these. How could Jesus make such a politically incorrect move as actually to eat with them?

Later in his gospel account, Luke will quote Jesus as saying, "For the Son of Man came to seek and to save the lost" (Luke 19:10). These are precisely the ones Jesus would want to eat with and talk with and laugh with and cry with and die with. So, it is probably with much glee that Luke clusters three "lost" parables in this "lost" chapter of the Bible. There are two, short anecdotal parables about a lost sheep and a lost coin, to which most people could relate. The gravity of being lost, however, is not fully sensed until the hearer enters the parable of the lost son, the prodigal one. Here Jesus is at his storytelling best.

This story has been worked and re-worked from just about every angle — the most familiar ones being that of the son, the father, and the elder brother. It might provide an interesting stretch of the imagination to relive the parable from the vantage point of the swine who shared the sty with this foreign species; or the harlots who helped him squander his money only to see him leave them more eager than he approached them, because he longed for more of what he truly needed; or the hired servants who observed all this and learned a great lesson on love from their master; or the friends who failed to go after him but were willing to celebrate his homecoming. What insights can be gained from an imaginative exploration of viewing this familiar story through unfamiliar eyes?

Application

It is rather sad to hear the reports on the state of health in America, notably how overweight we have become as a people, younger and older alike. Our consumption shows, in our over-sized garages and our over-sized waists. The manna of which we want more is not the true bread that feeds and nourishes us for life abundant and life eternal. Jesus, as the true bread that comes down from heaven (John 6:32-40), nourishes us in ways that keep us fit for daily life. The love that the father shows the errant son reflects the love of God through Jesus for us erring children; it is this love that fills us full of what we really want more of — acceptance, forgiveness, belonging, joy!

The manna was provisional for God's people as they wandered in the wilderness until that time when they were able to inhabit the land and work it for the fruit of the fields; so too is the Lord's Supper for God's people as they wander the four corners of the earth until eternity when they will share in the marriage feast of the lamb, the first fruit of all creation (see 1 Corinthians 15:20-28). There will be no need then for "more," because Christ will be all and in all (Colossians 1:15-21; 3:11).

There is a striking monument for peace in Ottowa, Canada. A solid wall rises out of the rubble of conflict. There are three figures on top, keeping vigilant watch. Etched in the stone is the word "reconciliation." Such a monument should be erected in Northern Ireland, Jerusalem, Yugoslavia, Africa, and Indonesia. With hot spots all over the world reminding us of our need for reconciliation, Paul's words strike a very contemporary note. The church can be present in any troubling situation with a clear word about God's intentions for our relationships: reconciliation. "We are ambassadors for Christ [entrusted with the message of reconciliation], God making his appeal through us" (2 Corinthians 5:20). The church today has inherited the mantel that Paul wore in his efforts to bring peace to the Corinthian congregation. We need to wear it boldly. That means publicly! Rather than thinking of our congregations as enclaves to shield us from the world, we should understand our congregations as platforms from which to dive into the affairs of the world with a word that can truly satisfy our concupiscence for more that propels us into power and boundary disputes. Because we know that human reconciliation is rooted in God's reconciliation with humanity (2 Corinthians 5:18), we dare not withhold this truth from the world.

This reconciliation can be worked out between nations as well as between people on the streets or within families. Would it be accurate to correlate the prodigal son's plight in the pig sty with the situation of street people in today's urban centers, whether in the United States, Germany, or Brazil? If so, how is the church today like the father waiting with open arms and an open heart when the lost one comes home smelling like a pig and dirtier than dirt? Are we ready with gospel hospitality to receive whoever comes to the door in whatever condition? Or, is the church like the elder brother with an attitude of preference? Do our congregations truly want to be filled with more "lost souls" or with more people "just like us"?

What good news there is for us all is that no one is so lost or so distant to make it impossible to return home to the heavenly Father! How remarkable upon reflection to be able to look back into our lostness and see how God's providential care was able to provide for us even then — like the nameless citizen who hired the prodigal and stood by him quietly until he came to his senses and then let him go from his hire to find the *more* he had been searching for all along.

Lent 5
Isaiah 43:16-21
Philippians 3:4b-14
John 12:1-8
David Kalas

Christian (version 7.0)

Personality tests, such as the Meyers-Briggs, will place two-word sets side by side and ask the participant to indicate a preference between the two. Without much time to think through all the nuances, the person using the device has to move quickly through the columns of words, sometimes agonizing and sometimes choosing easily.

Relying on reflex more than reflection, which of these two words do you prefer? *New. Old.*

Our preference varies with the situation, of course. We may long for a new house, while cherishing an old chair. We shop for a new computer to replace the old one, but we put it on the same old desk that we would never think of replacing. We buy a new sound system, and then we play our old music on it.

The people of God are always contending with issues of "new" and "old." In one circumstance, "old" means time-tested and proven. In another circumstance, it simply means outdated. For some, "new" means improved. For others, it connotes unorthodox.

Things old and new play major roles in our Old and New Testament lections for this week.

Isaiah 43:16-21

Keynote speakers are introduced by their resumes and bios. Whoever has the job of introducing the main speaker for some event usually has before him a vitae listing that speaker's accomplishments, qualities, and titles. For example:

Our special guest today is a renowned author... is CEO of such-and-such Fortune 500 company... is the pastor of the fastest growing church in America... is one of the foremost authorities on... has achieved unprecedented success in his field....

The audience's pump has been primed, and they wait with anticipation, eager to hear what this remarkable person has to say.

The prophet Isaiah, like a good emcee, has gone out of his way to introduce this word from the Lord by citing God's resume. Unwilling to simply pronounce — as he does in other places — "Thus says the Lord," followed by the prophecy, Isaiah makes a point of reminding his audience of God's past deeds. Specifically, Isaiah calls to mind the deliverance God provided for his people at the Red Sea in the days of Moses.

One would think that was a good approach. Speaking to a people in need of miraculous deliverance, it seems just right for Isaiah to recall aloud God's marvelous acts of deliverance on behalf of the people's ancestors. To a generation in captivity in a foreign land, Isaiah reminds the people how God saved an earlier generation from their captivity in a foreign land. He introduces God's word by citing God's credentials as a deliverer.

And then comes God's surprising word: "Forget about it."

All those past accomplishments, the marvelous stories that are Israel's testimony, the signs and wonders of old — God instructs the people to set them aside and not to give them a second thought.

It's an astonishing command coming from the God who typically exhorts his people to remember — that is, to recall, ritually and regularly, God's saving deeds from days gone by. But not now. Now, in the moment when deliverance is needed again, God urges his people to forget what he has done in the past.

I suppose it is an irksome thing for a musician to have concert crowds wanting only to hear the old favorites. If the artist or band has been around for a while, and if their songs have become cherished oldies to a generation of fans, it is almost impossible to introduce a new song. The concertgoers are so emotionally attached to the old stuff that any new songs are almost unwelcome.

So it is oftentimes between God and God's people. We have so fallen in love with some "hit" from long ago. It meant so much to us at the time and new layers of fond and sentimental attachment have been added with each passing year. We may be unwittingly unwilling, as a result, to let God do a new and different thing in our lives.

And so God urged the people of Isaiah's day to stow away their old 45s — those well-worn records singing of what God had done in the days of Moses, Joshua, or David. He was coming out with a new hit, and he wanted his people to be prepared to hear it and to sing and dance along with it.

Philippians 3:4b-14

The standard magician will startle his audience by seeming to destroy something precious or valuable. Here is a legal tender $50 bill that seems to be torn in pieces or set on fire. Here is an expensive wristwatch or piece of jewelry that seems to have been crushed or to have disappeared altogether. And here is a real, live human being that seems to have been cut in two.

The sleight of hand has more impact because the thing involved has value. Few audiences would watch wide-eyed if a performer appeared to saw a log in two and put it back together. No one would gasp at a cheap thing being set on fire.

Paul invites a gasp from the Philippian audience in this passage. He trots out something of great value, and then seems to make that thing vanish before their eyes.

The thing of value, in this case, is Paul's proud past.

In our materialistic world, where people are judged more by what they have than by who they are, Paul's heritage may go unappreciated. But Paul came from a world — and wrote, at least in part, to a people — for which the great measure in life was not possessions but the law. When Paul set himself against that measure, the measure of the law, the audience was impressed.

On the one hand, there are the matters that Paul could take no credit for personally. His unblemished Jewish pedigree included his tribe, his circumcision according to the law, and his Hebrew parentage.

On the other hand, there were those matters for which Paul could take credit.

First, he was a Pharisee. That does not sound like a favorable claim in the ears of most of our people, for all we know of Pharisees is some of what Jesus said about them. In this context, however, we must recognize that the Pharisees were the most devoutly religious and most carefully obedient men of that day in Israel. Jesus' issue with the Pharisees was their hypocrisy, but there is no indication that hypocrisy was a problem for Paul. He was, we gather, an impeccably pious man.

Second, there was Paul's zeal. His was not a mind-your-own-business religiosity. No, he was a crusader, a zealot, a man of holy indignation who sought to do right and to right wrongs. And, up until his conversion on the road to Damascus, the wrong he sought to right was that seemingly heretical movement within Judaism involving the followers of Jesus. In his passionate obedience to God, Paul endeavored to shut up and shut down the heretics.

Finally, there was Paul's most remarkable claim: he was blameless. Who can make a claim like that? Yet Paul had weighed himself in the balance of the law and found that he was not wanting.

Then comes the moment when Paul takes the saw or the fire to these things of value. "Whatever gains I had, these I have come to regard as loss... I regard them as rubbish." *This thing I treasured...? Watch me crumple it up and throw it away. This thing of great value...? See how I put it down the disposal, run it through the shredder, toss it in the garbage.*

31

A materialistic world may not value the same things that Paul did, but we do value things. And we can be certain that Paul's response to our things of value would be precisely the same. *Watch me throw it all away.*

The shock and strength of what Paul says is found best in the Greek word *skubalon*, translated here "rubbish." The King James Version translates it "dung." We might think of still other words. The very stuff that Paul was so proud of previously, he can't wait to scrape off the bottom of his shoe. He is eager to shake it loose and leave it behind, for he has found something so much better.

Here is where Paul and the standard magician part company. The audience is shocked when the large bill is set on fire but relieved to find that it somehow survived. The audience is startled to see a living person cut in half but delighted to see that apparent victim in one piece when the trick is over.

Paul, however, does not reassemble the thing of value. He leaves it burned, cut, and shredded. What he wants his Philippian audience to see is not the magic of the valuable thing restored, but the testimony of the valuable thing cast aside — cast aside in favor of "the surpassing value of knowing Christ Jesus my Lord."

John 12:1-8

This dinner must have been a come-as-you-are affair, for that's surely how everyone came. In just a few descriptive verses, John gives us a glimpse around the table, and we discover that everyone looks very familiar.

First, there is Martha being Martha.

Most of us would be able to predict within our own family gatherings who is likely to do what. At our extended family's Christmas celebration, for example, I could predict to you who will arrive early and who will arrive late. We know who is going to carve the turkey, who is going to hand out the presents, and who is going to be continually getting up from the table to make sure that everyone has what he or she needs.

Likewise, when you ate dinner at the home of Mary, Martha, and Lazarus, you could bet that Martha was going to serve. The gospel of Luke (10:38-42) provides us with the famous episode that makes this account ring so true. Martha fusses away at making preparations, while Mary neglects the housework in favor of sitting and listening to Jesus. Martha does not compare favorably in that passage. In the larger business of the kingdom and of Jesus' teachings, however, we must evaluate Martha generously. Serving, after all, is the great hallmark of the follower of Jesus (see Matthew 23:11; Luke 12:35-40, 17:7-10, 22:27; John 12:26; Philippians 2:5-7). Serving is the essence of greatness in the kingdom (Matthew 20:25-28). And serving is how Martha loved — a vital missing element from so much of what passes for love in our day.

Next, there is Mary being Mary.

As we mentioned before, Luke offers the quintessential character profile of Mary and Martha in Jesus' visit to their home in chapter 10. As in that passage, Mary is again at Jesus' feet (Luke 10:39; John 12:3). Mary is the portrait of worship: at Jesus' feet, attentive and adoring.

Next, there is Judas being Judas.

Folks in my generation will likely remember the rock opera *Jesus Christ Superstar*. This episode from John's gospel appears early in that musical account of Jesus' final days. A friend and I were joking recently that *Jesus Christ Superstar* might better have been titled *Judas Iscariot: Tragic Hero*, for the psyche of Judas seems to be the real issue of the piece. Judas is depicted as a tortured but well-intentioned tragic figure, which is a much more flattering portrayal than the one the gospel writer offers us.

John shows us a Judas who is not only a thief, but also a thief who deliberately veils his vice under the guise of humanitarian concern. The embezzler dares to condemn the worshiper for misappropriation of funds. The wicked one pretends the indignation of the righteous.

We are well acquainted with the thirty pieces of silver Judas was paid for betraying Jesus. It's hard to imagine that such an average sum would drive a man to such epic treachery. Such is the intoxication of money, however, and when we live under its influence, we lose our judgment and proper reflexes. So it is that no one can serve both God and money (Matthew 6:24), hard as we may try.

When Judas looks at an act of worship but only sees dollar signs, we simply observe Judas being Judas.

Perhaps the question to ask is whether we also see ourselves.

Next, there is Lazarus being, well, there.

Lazarus is the only individual at this dinner who is named but not described as doing or saying anything. We know what both Mary and Martha did. We know what both Judas and Jesus said. All that we know about Lazarus, however, is that he was there. And that is enough, for he was a living testimony to the power of Christ. It was only one chapter earlier that Lazarus was bound and foul in the tomb, his sisters bereaved, and Jesus at a distance. Now, however, the whole group of friends and siblings is seated together around a table, full of life and joy.

Finally, there is Jesus being Jesus. He is the one who comes and sups with us (Revelation 3:20). He is the one who corrects and challenges us (John 12:7-8). He is the one at whose feet we bow down and worship (John 12:3).

Application

A computerized generation understands the language of upgrades and new versions of old software. The latest Pentium makes us wonder how we ever got anything done with our old computer. The newest, biggest, sharpest flat screen makes our old monitor seem intolerable. All the things that this new version of a program or operating system can do makes the earlier version obsolete.

Why would we choose to hold onto that which is slower, weaker, and less productive? Why wouldn't we toss aside the outdated and inadequate version for the new and improved one?

Historically, however, the people of God have resisted upgrades.

Sometimes the people of God have wanted to retreat to the past because the future seemed too frightening (Numbers 14:3-4). Sometimes they have so cherished the past that it became idolatrous (2 Kings 18:4). Sometimes they have allowed "past good" to morph into "only good" (Luke 5:36-39).

The people of Isaiah's day, however, were challenged not to "remember the former things or consider the things of old." Those former things were not bad, mind you. They were glorious deeds of God and part of Israel's testimony. But with their eyes fixed on the rearview mirror, God's people were apt to miss what he had for them down the road. "I am about to do a new thing; now it springs forth, do you not perceive it?"

Paul, meanwhile, declared that he had indeed set aside the former things. He was no longer finding glory in the old things, but rather "forgetting what lies behind and straining forward to what lies ahead, I press on toward the goal...."

So it is that we are presented with a God who does new things, and who invites us into new things.

Now I believe that the pulpit is too important to be used as a proprietary weapon during in-house battles. The truth at stake in these lections is more profound than local church squabbles between new styles and old traditions. The issue at hand is not superficial questions of style and taste. Rather, the issue is a God who was offering something better than what Isaiah's contemporaries had known to date; a God who offered something better than what Paul had known before; and a God who, very likely, has something better for us — individually and corporately — than what we have experienced thus far. Our scriptural challenge is not to keep up with the times, the fashions, or the technology. Our real challenge is to keep up with God.

Alternative Applications

John 12:1-8. We illustrated above the characteristic differences between the two sisters, Mary and Martha. Differences can be embraced or resisted in our congregations. How you and I are different may be a cherished source of celebration or a bitter point of constant tension.

Our churches will be healthier and happier if we leave room — make room — for the different ways people love and serve the Lord. I'm not a proponent of "anything goes." But one of the lovely truths of this passage is that Mary and Martha were different types of people, and so naturally they manifested their love and service in different ways. Martha was the one always on her feet. Mary, by contrast, was the one always on her knees.

I see Mary and Martha in this scene and I am reminded of the Hebrew word *abad*. A comparison of a few translations of Psalm 100:2 will reveal the beauty of this word. The King James and Revised Standard Versions offer the familiar translation, "Serve the Lord with gladness." The New International and New Revised Standard Versions, meanwhile, translate the phrase, "Worship the Lord with gladness."

What a discovery to find that worshiping and serving God are not separate acts. To worship him is to serve him and to serve him is to worship him. While Martha serves the Lord with gladness, Mary worships him with gladness.

Perhaps in our churches from time to time, Martha needs to be challenged to a deeper devotional life while Mary is encouraged to leave the prayer group and help out in the kitchen every once in a while. Most of the time, though, Mary and Martha should be blessed and embraced for how they each serve and worship the Lord with gladness.

John 12:1-8. Different congregations celebrate the sacrament of communion at different times. If your congregation will be partaking of the sacrament together on this Sunday, perhaps the passage from John would provide a good opportunity to work with the motif of dining with Jesus.

Dining with Jesus is a personal thing — a symbol of his grace toward us and his friendship and fellowship with us. This homey episode with the family of Mary, Martha, and Lazarus is a good picture. So, too, the way Jesus invited himself to eat with Zacchaeus (Luke 19:5) and the way he awaits our invitation to have him sup with us (Revelation 3:20).

Dining with Jesus is also a celebrative thing. Surely it was a happy occasion for Lazarus and his sisters to have Jesus back in their home following the miraculous events of the previous chapter. One senses, too, that the meal with Zacchaeus was a happy occasion. We also see Jesus at the wedding feast in Cana (John 2:1-12). And the dining we do with Jesus here is only a foretaste of the festive celebration that will be the great banquet in the kingdom (see Matthew 26:29; Luke 14:15-24).

Dining with Jesus is also a sacramental thing. It is an occasion of worship for Mary (John 12:3), of epiphany for the disciples in Emmaus (Luke 24:28-35), and of God's presence and grace for his believers in every generation (1 Corinthians 11:23-26).

The tipping point

In his book, *The Tipping Point*, Malcolm Gladwell shows how some events and activities take on a life of their own when they pass a critical mark. Up until that point, the context can be managed and the outcomes determined. But once something reaches the tipping point, everything changes and energies snowball into effects that cannot be contained.

A friend sent me a series of pictures that displayed the tipping point humorously. At a small seaside town in British Columbia, a small car careened carelessly on waterfront streets and ended ignobly by tipping off a pier into the briny. Rescuers brought in their crane truck to extend its boom over the partially submerged vehicle, planning to winch it up onto the pavement again. A local photographer captured their efforts as the weight of the soggy sedan overloaded the lifting capacity of the crane and it too tipped into the water, landing squarely on top of its object of rescue.

The tale refused to end because town officials gathered in worry and brought in a much larger crane truck from a neighboring village. This behemoth had large extenders that planted stabilizing feet at a secure distance from its frame and a boom built like a giant's claw. With confidence, the operators snaked a hook to lift the fallen smaller truck back from its baptismal shame. Then, just as brutish force seemed invincible, the leeward stabilizers picked themselves up from the pavement and the monster truck gracefully eased into its own tipping point and pirouetted in an arc onto its lesser cousins below. What a tragedy for the machines and their owners but what a terrific day for the photographer!

The lectionary readings for today are all focused on the tipping point of Jesus' final week in Jerusalem. Isaiah pictures it from a distance, anticipating the suffering servant's dialogue with the Father as he enters the dark journey of unjust punishment buoyed only by divine favor. Paul poetically traces the parabola of Jesus' obedient descent to the cross which, in turn, energizes his triumphant ascent back to glory, and Luke takes us from the Last Supper to the supposed last resting place as Jesus is careened among the architects of his death in the final hours of Passion Week. This is the biblical tipping point. Because of it everything changes.

Isaiah 50:4-9a

These verses are found in what is often identified as Second Isaiah (40-55), where judgment and salvation are synthesized in magnificent pictures of grace. These masterpieces are then further interwoven around the mysterious figure of the suffering servant. While it is hard to fully understand Isaiah's vision in his own context (Is the nation of Israel the "suffering servant"? Or perhaps Judah? Is it possibly an enigmatic deliverer from David's royal family? Or even a composite character created for heroic encouragement during Judah's dark times? Is there a historical manifestation of these paradoxical scenes of misplaced identity and deliverance?), there seems to be so much clarity when allowing them to foreshadow Jesus.

There are few good ways to exegete this passage so that it rings true in Isaiah's context and also speaks clearly about the Christ of Passion Week. Perhaps the best homiletic move would be to refer to these verses in snippets of supportive commentary undergirding explorations of Jesus' unjust treatment, using them as insight into the psychological dialogue between the Son and Father. While the world pummels the sinless Christ externally, assuming all manner of self-justified attacks against this outsider, an interior and private conversation might unfold along these lines as Jesus fulfills a redemptive destiny beyond society's ken.

Philippians 2:5-11

Philippians is one of Paul's prison letters, written from Rome around 60 AD while Paul was under house arrest waiting to fulfill his appeal to Caesar (see Acts 26-28). It is one of his most joy-filled letters (along with 1 Thessalonians, written about a decade earlier). This is somewhat amazing since Luke's record of the beginnings of the congregations in Acts 16 would not initially suggest a warm and loving fellowship. Its original members were the strong and independent business woman Lydia, the wispy and spiritually empathic fortune-teller slave girl, and the battle-hardened, retired Roman legionnaire pensioned off to a bit of property in the neighborhood that happened to have a cave he turned into a mercenary incarceration pit. Nevertheless, the congregation that grew from the witness of these became one of Paul's favorites, and he stopped there often in his travels.

Most of our Bibles arrange these verses in poetic form, for the text certainly has the feel of a verse. Scholars often identify this as an early hymn of the church. Perhaps it was written by Paul, or perhaps it was a popular song of faith that he incorporated into his message. In any case it forms a balanced summary of Christ's incarnation and coronation. Care must be taken not to divorce it from its lead-in. Paul uses the hymn in a particular way, as an incentive to mutual submission and humble service within the congregation (vv. 1-4). Thus, while we often abstract the theological statement to confirm our Christological doctrinal statements, we need also to see the ethical impact it has for Christian behavior.

In this way, minor incidents must not detract us from the sweeping momentum of the divine mandate. We view the life of Jesus at the nadir of its parabolic swoop, feeling with him the crunch of a hammer release in full collision with its intended mark. All the energy expended to carry the second person of the Trinity across the gulf between heaven and earth, and raise up this agent of divine grace, is pounding Jesus into the final confines of submission. What began as a shout of angels near Bethlehem is now whimpering into the bloody torment of Calvary. With Paul, we are eager to rush ahead to the victory shout of "Jesus is Lord!"; with Paul, we must also first linger in depths of Jesus' "obedience unto death."

As with the Isaiah passage, this hymn of faith is not so much to be preached but to be sung or emoted. What would one feel while processing through this roller coaster of social upset? How does Jesus find himself fully engaged in the degrading process of betrayal, denial, misunderstanding, and religious ostracism, especially when it appears that he is limited from knowing with clarity the full victory that will come and wrestles painfully with the Father about this challenge while praying in Gethsemane garden?

It is in this context that Paul gives the brief poetic exhortation about the characteristics that mark those on Jesus' team. It is not self-preservation but service that counts. It is not superiority but selflessness that wins points. It is not stridency but sacrifice that finds recognition from the owner of the club. Jesus is building a team that will change the world. Unfortunately on that day, too few people seemed willing to show up at the try-outs.

There is a scene in Tolkien's *The Fellowship of the Ring* where a partnership is forged among those who would accompany Frodo on his journey to destroy the ring of power. The movie version makes for a very gripping visual illustration, and the original literary text is equally as moving. What comes through is a sense of selflessness as the bond that unites these creatures. Furthermore, each subsumes his will to the greater cause and trusts an unseen and transcendent good for an outcome that will bless all of Middle Earth, even if the trek itself causes the demise of any or all of the compatriots.

So it is in Paul's small glimpse of Jesus working out the mission of God. In a world turned cold to its Creator, in an age riddled by Delphic oracles, temple prostitutes, and emperors claiming divinity, in a little corner of geography where messianic hopes ran high, God called together a strange team to make its mark by playing a different game.

Walter Wangerin Jr., in his great allegory, *The Book of the Dun Cow* (along with its wonderful sequel, *The Book of Sorrows*), captures the scope of the divine mission as well as the underrated character of the team. If the focus remains on the team apart from the mission, the point is lost. God is reclaiming God's creation but does so through human agency. The game is fierce and the playing field is rough. Only those who can tear up their personal score sheets in order to get into God's game will make the team. Only they are truly called. Only they are equipped to serve, follow, and play on the greatest winning team of all time.

Luke 22:14—23:56

How should we preach this entire narrative? It is impossible to dwell adequately on each important segment — the table scene with both its Lord's Supper institution and the disciples' self-importance squabbles, prayers in the garden, the betrayal and arrest and denials, the mockings, sham trials, and crucifixion. Either a specific passage has to become the source of homiletic development, or some metaphor needs to cull the main themes and present them in a gripping manner.

One approach that serves the latter method is an allegory developed by Walter Wangerin Jr. in which Jesus is called the Ragman. Wangerin pictures himself in a city on a Friday morning. A handsome young man comes to town, dragging behind him a cart made of wood. The cart is piled high with new, clean clothes, bright and shiny and freshly pressed.

Wandering through the streets the trader marches, crying out his strange deal: "Rags! New rags for old! Give me your old rags, your tired rags, your torn and soiled rags!"

He sees a woman on the back porch of a house. She is old and tired and weary of living. She has a dirty handkerchief pressed to her nose, and she is crying 1,000 tears, sobbing over the pains of her life.

The Ragman takes a clean linen handkerchief from his wagon and brings it to the woman. He lays it across her arm. She blinks at him, wondering what he is up to. Gently, the young man opens her fingers and releases the old, dirty, soaking handkerchief from her knotted fist.

Then comes the wonder. The Ragman touches the old rag to his own eyes and begins to weep her tears. Meanwhile, behind him on her porch stands the old woman, tears gone, eyes full of peace.

It happens again. "New rags for old!" he cries, and he comes to a young girl wearing a bloody bandage on her head. He takes the caked and soiled wrap away and gives her a new bonnet from his cart. Then he wraps the old rags around his head. As he does this, the girl's cuts disappear and her skin turns rosy. She dances away with laughter and returns to her friends to play. But the Ragman begins to moan and from her rags on his head the blood spills down.

He next meets a man. "Do you have a job?" the Ragman asks. With a sneer the man replies, "Are you kidding?" and holds up his shirtsleeve. There is no arm in it. He cannot work. He is disabled.

But the Ragman says, "Give me your shirt. I'll give you mine."

The man's shirt hangs limp as he takes it off, but the Ragman's shirt hangs firm and full because one of the Ragman's arms is still in the sleeve. It goes with the shirt. When the man puts it on, he has a new arm. The Ragman walks away with one sleeve dangling.

It happens over and over again. The Ragman takes the clothes from the tired, the hurting, the lost, and the lonely. He gathers them to his own body and takes the pains into his own heart. Then he gives new clothes to new lives with new purpose and new joy.

Finally, around midday, the Ragman finds himself at the center of the city where nothing remains but a stinking garbage heap. It is the accumulated refuse of a society lost to anxiety and torture. On Friday afternoon, the Ragman climbs the hill, stumbling as he drags his cart behind him. He is tired and sore and pained and bleeding. He falls on the wooden beams of the cart, alone and dying from the disease and disaster he has garnered from others.

Wangerin wonders at the sight. In exhaustion and uncertainty, he falls asleep. He lies dreaming nightmares through all of Saturday, until he is shaken from his fitful slumbers early on Sunday morning. The ground quakes. Wangerin looks up. In surprise he sees the Ragman stand up. He is alive! The sores are gone, though the scars remain. But the Ragman's clothes are new and clean. Death has been swallowed up and transformed by life!

Still worn and troubled in his spirit, Wangerin cries up to the Ragman, "Dress me, Ragman! Give me your clothes to wear! Make me new!"

We know the picture. It is the one Luke unfolds here. Jesus is the Ragman who must touch lives, who must heal wounds, who is bound by necessity to bring relief. This is the pilgrimage of the Ragman to the center of the city, to the garbage heap of society, to the hill called Golgotha — the skull! The place of death! The mountain of the crucifixion! There he must go. Personally.

But so, too, those who are with him, including the disciples in his day and all who come to faith through their testimony. That is why Jesus speaks so pointedly in addressing the squabbles of the Last Supper. Religion is neither an individual game nor a spectator sport. Harry Emerson Fosdick remembered a storm off the Atlantic coast. A ship foundered on the rocks and the Coast Guard was called out. The captain ordered the lifeboat to be launched, but one of the crew members protested. "Sir," he said in fear, "the wind is offshore and the tide is running out! We can launch the boat, but we'll never get back!"

The captain looked at him with a father's eyes, and then said, "Launch the boat, men. We have to go out. That is our duty. But we don't have to come back." This is the tipping point for those who follow Jesus on the road of discipleship.

Application

The Cost of Discipleship, as Dietrich Bonhoeffer noted, is self-denial, and today's lectionary passages clearly point to Jesus' life as a strong call for us to join him in that vocation, not as an end in itself or as a means to a self-help goal (like dieting), but rather as a countercultural missional testimony. Those who travel this road do not get to Easter without first enduring Good Friday; they do not presume a glorious outcome that gathers the media like paparazzi vultures, but sense that the journey of service brings light in darkness, hope in despair, healing for pain, and faith where power corrupts and destroys.

An Alternative Application

Luke 22:14—23:56. The gospel lesson invites us to focus special attention on the person of Peter. Jesus singles him out for a special exhortation. In spite of himself, Peter was about to take the easy way out precisely at the point where Jesus was about to go through the hardest part of his journey. Peter wanted to save his own life, and in so doing deny himself a place on Jesus' team. Yet after these events, Peter learned some great lessons that make a wonderful illustration to bring home the discipleship impact of the Passion story. According to stories from the early church, at the time of the intense persecution under Nero, the Christians of Rome told Peter to leave. "You're too valuable," they said. "Get out of town! Find your safety! Go to another place and preach the gospel."

According to legend, Peter is supposed to have gone from the city. Yet, only a few days later, Nero had Peter in custody. Soon afterward, he was sent out to die. When the soldiers took Peter to the site of execution, Peter begged of them one last request. He asked that he might be crucified upside down. He said he wasn't worthy to die in the same way as his Lord. So they nailed him to his cross inverted.

According to the stories, the crowds of Christians gathered round. They wanted to be with their beloved leader as he died. "Why," they asked him as he hung there upside down on the cross, "why did you come back, Father Peter? Why did you return to Rome? Why didn't you flee into the hills?"

This is what Peter is supposed to have said. "When you told me to leave the city, I made my escape. But as I was going down the road, I met our Lord Jesus. He was walking back toward Rome, so I asked him, 'Master, where are you going?' He said to me, 'I am going to the city to be crucified.' 'But, Lord,' I responded, 'were you not crucified once for all?' And he said to me, 'I saw you fleeing from death and now I wish to be crucified instead of you.' Then I knew what I must do. 'Go, Lord!' I told him. 'I will finish my pilgrimage.' And he said to me, 'Fear not, for I am with you.' "

Maundy Thursday
Exodus 12:1-4 (5-10) 11-14
1 Corinthians 11:23-26
John 13:1-17, 31b-35
Mark Molldrem

Dutiful servants of all

Do we ever really get together anymore? Think about it. Funeral homes are experimenting with drive-through visitation. In order to make an uncomfortable situation less awkward, one can now avoid looking into the eyes of a child whose parents just got a divorce — instead, send them a greeting card designed for just such an occasion. TV trays can be set up more easily than setting the kitchen table, and this way everyone can take care of themselves when it is convenient. Teleconferences give a whole new meaning to "calling a meeting."

Even though services are provided over the phone or on the internet or through the mail to people by people who never meet in person, one still wonders what is missing when we can live so much of our lives without rubbing shoulders with others. As we enter the Triduum of Holy Week, we cannot escape noticing how "hands on" everything becomes for God when dealing with humanity. The incarnation bears its ripest fruit in these final hours of Jesus' lifelong passion.

The gospel writer John does not let us escape noticing that the message Jesus leaves with his disciples is one that can only be expressed when they are gathered together. No memos, instant messaging, or call forwarding are used to convey what is on the heart of God. It is communicated only when the disciples are within reach of Jesus, and then within reach of one another. One may be able to play solitaire with cards but not with Christianity.

Exodus 12:1-4 (5-10) 11-14

When the Lord promised to redeem the 'Apiru slaves in Egypt "with an out-stretched arm and with great acts of judgment" (Exodus 6:6), no one thought of counting just how many acts it would take nor that when the count reached nine, it would only take one more devastating blow to the pride of Pharaoh to make him relent and let God's people go. As with most of the plagues, this tenth one would not touch the Israelites, providing they took drastic action — an action, the likes of which they did *not* need to take to be spared the previous plagues.

A sacrifice needed to be made. A spotless lamb was to be selected for each house. After the lamb was slain, its blood was to be sprinkled over the doorposts and lintel of the house. When the assigned angel of death crossed over the land to execute God's judgment, the angel would pass over the homes of the Israelites on which the blood had been sprinkled. Some important and enduring concepts undergird this requirement and the *eat and run* Passover meal that resulted.

First, a sacrifice was understood as necessary in order to protect God's people from his wrath. Life needed to be shed in order to preserve life. Since "the life is in the blood," it made sense to sprinkle the blood upon the doorposts and lintel as the sign that the appropriate sacrifice had been made. This gesture was sacrificial in that it was substitutionary for the firstborn male, who would be the object of God's wrath due to Pharaoh's hardness of heart.

Second, God himself provided the means of escape from the wrath to come. God would acknowledge and accept the blood of the lamb (or goat) and *pass over* the home that by faith had obeyed the command. God is not capricious or careless when it comes to the implementation of his response to human rebellion or need. The love and care of God for his people is expressed in this arrangement.

Third, the Passover is to be observed as an ordinance forever. The meal not only solemnizes the event at the time; but, for all time, it becomes the means by which future generations are connected to what happened in Egypt at this particular time. In this sense, the meal is a *remembrance*, not just recollecting what occurred as an intellectual exercise, but participating in its meaning and experiencing the power of God's deliverance in the here and now.

Fourth, time itself is reordered based upon this event. "This month shall be for you the beginning of months; it shall be the first month of the year for you" (12:1). Historically, this is the constituting event of the people of God, who from this point in time could reflect back upon the call of Abraham and even creation itself to find the beginnings of all these things that are taking place. See Deuteronomy 6:21-23 and 26:5-9 as examples of creedal/confessional statements of self-understanding. Although a half-century old and firmly couched in the historical-critical method, B. Davie Napier's *Song of the Vineyard* offers a refreshing and insightful explication of this and other first covenant events with their meanings.

1 Corinthians 11:23-26

Paul's discussion of the Lord's Supper is found in the section of his first letter to the Corinthian congregation in which he deals with matters of public worship. There is an issue pertaining to the veiling of women that needs to be addressed. Paul asserts the tradition of women needing to veil their heads when it comes to prayer and prophecy. In a more lengthy treatment, Paul turns his attention to spiritual gifts, which was another source of contention in the congregation. He identifies the source of these gifts in God, their variety for the common good of edification, and the highest gift of all — love. In the midst of these matters, Paul instructs the Corinthians regarding proper behavior at the Lord's Supper.

As with so many other things they did in their Christian life, the Corinthian Christians messed up when it came to their experience with the Lord's Supper. They did not sit at table together, but some ate early. That meant that others, who came in later, went hungry. The ones who started without the others imbibed too much and profaned the meal. The congregation suffered from gluttony and lack of a "potluck" mentality (where there is always enough for everyone because all share what they have!).

It is within this context that the words that come after our assigned text are to be understood. "Discerning the body" (11:29) refers to a healthy appreciation of every member of the congregation and being sensitive to how each is to be included in the meal. The reference to "the body and blood of the Lord" (11:27) refers directly to the elements. Later, Paul mentions frailties of the body (physical; "weak and ill," 11:30), from which some have died. Here are three different senses of the word "body" reflected in these few verses.

These things having been said, we can now look at the core of this section on public worship that deals with the Lord's Supper. Paul reminds the Corinthians what is at the heart of the Lord's Supper. This is not shared as the "correct theology" of the elements, as if what was at stake here was a kind of proper mantra, without which one would participate "in an unworthy manner" (11:27). The matter of unworthiness has already been discussed in terms of their behavior at the meal. What Paul does here in these few verses is ground the meal in Jesus and lift up its intention.

First, Paul makes the claim that what he expresses here now is "received from the Lord" (11:23). Although Paul was not present with the other disciples at the original Maundy Thursday event, he asserts apostolic authority in what he outlines as the *main course* of the meal. Jesus is at the center of the meal, for it is his body and his blood that are shared. In this sense, he is the author of the meal and focus is to be on him. This alone should curb inappropriate behaviors!

Second, the congregation is reminded through the words of Jesus that the meal is indeed "for you" (11:24). Martin Luther personalized this in Latin when he referred so thankfully to the *pro me* nature of the sacrament. What Jesus is doing in the Passover meal is redefining it around the deliverance that he offers

God's people (the new Israel represented in the twelve apostles) through his body sacrificed and his blood shed to avert the wrath of God upon the ungodly. To borrow John's words, we discover in Jesus "the lamb of God who takes away the sins of the world" (John 1:29). The writer of the letter to the Hebrews draws the connection between Jesus and the entire sacrificial system with these words: "For if the sprinkling of defiled persons with the blood of goats and bulls and with the ashes of a heifer sanctifies for the purification of the flesh, how much more shall the blood of Christ, who through the eternal Spirit offered himself without blemish to God, purify your conscience from dead works to serve the living God" (Hebrews 9:13-14).

Third, the meaning of the meal is to "proclaim the Lord's death until he come" (11:26). It is not about "getting your fill" or "tying one on at the end of a hard day." The meal is a living, dramatic sermon to the world that "Christ has died, Christ is risen, Christ will come again!" The meal proclaims what God has already done in Jesus Christ (that is why Matthew includes the words "for the forgiveness of sins" in his account; Matthew 26:28!) and what Jesus has yet to do, namely return. In the meantime, the church watches and waits while it works for the kingdom's goals. One might say that this makes the Lord's Supper a *wait and work* meal, rather than the *eat and run* meal of the Passover.

The Words of Institution used in the liturgies of the meal are essentially a compilation of this text in 1 Corinthians 11 and the account in Matthew 26. The Passover meal is transformed into a sacrament for the church with the reinterpretation of its meaning. The deliverance from bondage to Pharaoh presages deliverance from bondage to sin. Blood is present at both events: the first from a spotless lamb and the second from the spotless lamb of God. "Indeed, under the law almost everything is purified with blood, and without the shedding of blood there is no forgiveness of sins" (Hebrews 9:22).

John 13:1-17, 31b-35

The account of Jesus washing the disciples' feet is one of the distinctive features that sets John's gospel apart from the synoptic gospels. Rather than recording the meal in detail, with emphasis on the transformation of the Passover meal to the Lord's Supper, John simply mentions that they ate. In fact, the supper itself is overshadowed by what Jesus does. He disrobes and assumes the role of the servant, washing the disciples' feet.

Surrounding this episode are comments by Jesus on himself as light (12:44-50, before) and "the way, the truth and the life" (14:1-7, after). By washing the disciples' feet, Jesus sought to illuminate their understanding about true love and leadership. It is a matter of humble service (13:16-17). The *doulov* (slave, servant) is under the *kuriov* (master, lord). Therefore, if the master himself, Jesus, whom the disciples call *Kuriov*, washes feet, then, the disciples (as *doulov*) should also do so. Jesus exemplifies how he wants his followers to exercise their love and leadership in the world — through humble service. "I have given you an example that you also should do as I have done to you" (13:15). This is "the way, and the truth, and the life" for anyone who would find themselves in Jesus.

When Jesus defines his commandment given to his disciples in terms of love, the best word to translate that reality is *ûgapj* (13:34-35). Four times this word is used in these two verses. Paul may go on about the qualities of love, as he does in 1 Corinthians 13. John simply portrays it through this simple, yet profound act lived out by Jesus under the shadow of his cross. The foot washing foreshadows the cross because both have to do with cleansing — the one from the dirt of the road and the other from the sin of the journey.

Martin Luther, in his little tract *Christian Liberty*, writes, "A Christian is a perfectly free lord of all, subject to none. A Christian is a perfectly dutiful servant of all, subject to all." As we are free *from* sin, so we are free *for* service. Because we are the lords of life (both with and without the apostrophe), we are called upon to serve the needs of the world wherever we may find them. It is never too humbling a task to "devote all our works to the welfare of others, since each has such abundant riches in his faith that all his other works and his whole life are a surplus with which he can by voluntary benevolence serve and do good to his neighbor," as Luther would write. When one pictures Jesus stooping to wash the disciples' feet in devotion to the mission on which his heavenly Father sent him, these words of Luther apply not only to him, but also to any who would follow him likewise: "By faith he is caught up beyond himself into God. By love he descends beneath himself into his neighbor." This is the witness of love and this is how the Father is glorified.

Application

It is interesting to see that *Habits of the Heart*, published in the mid-'80s, has been reprinted with an extended introduction, claiming that the American ethos of individualism is very much functioning as a defining character of our identity. Once studied, it does not go away. Our sense of "rugged individualism" is ingrained into our character, despite so much of our altruism and education that seeks to balance it. In this context, the Passover meal and Holy Communion provide a story that sets before us a different model with which to understand ourselves. The Passover was a household meal; Holy Communion, where two or three are gathered. The essential social characters of both Judaism and Christianity invite us to be engaged in relationships that are necessary for nurture. The relationships are both to the story itself as participants in faith, as well as to other people who hold the value of the story in expressing the meaning of their lives.

The "for you" aspect of the sacrament emphasizes that something has been done on our behalf. This is something we could not do on our own, namely forgive our sins and overcome death. The crucified and risen Lord Jesus strides to meet us at the communion rail with the assurance that he has done just that "for you." As unilateral as that action of grace is, so too are we invited to receive it in faith. We do this by participating in the meal — from gathering with others, to voicing the liturgical words that articulate the meaning of the meal, to receiving the food itself, to going out into the world together as witnesses of what we have just received from the hand of God.

In the busy routines of daily life where families find precious little time to get together, especially for meals, the church can ring the dinner bell. As the people of God assemble, there is time to hear the story that constitutes faith and life; there is time to build relationships upon the solid foundation, not so much on what we can do for each other, but on what God has done for us all through our Lord Jesus Christ. Because while the meal is *for us*, it is *about* Jesus Christ. As we feast on him and the gospel meat he gives us to savor, we receive each other as fellow servants who have learned from the same Master. Ecumenism, as well as neighborliness, could make great strides forward if we all understood better what it means to wash feet rather than wring necks.

The people nearby

You know the experience of showing photographs to someone who was not part of the trip, or group, or event where the pictures were taken. You walk the other person through each photograph. You describe what the occasion was, where the place was, and who the people were.

Today may offer an opportunity to do just that again. Today, Good Friday, the pictures we sit down and look at together are from the passion of Christ.

We have three different pictures to view. Isaiah, John, and the writer of Hebrews all have their own portraits of the event.

John's camera, if you will, is more a movie camera than a still-shot camera. His pictures move us from place to place, as we follow Jesus from the Last Supper to the garden, then to the trials before the council and the governor, then up to Golgotha, and then to the tomb.

The writer of Hebrews, meanwhile, offers more of a still shot of the event. Specifically, he takes the picture of Christ on Good Friday up against the backdrop of the Old Testament law, with its rituals, priests, sacrifices, and blood.

Finally, the prophet Isaiah's picture of the occasion is sort of a collage. An assortment of images is employed in the Old Testament text: a variety of pieces that are arranged together to form a single whole.

We sit down today to look at these pictures together. We see the occasion: Christ's suffering and death. We also recognize the place involved in these pictures: Jerusalem, Gethsemane, a hill called "skull," and a nearby tomb. Then, finally, there are the assorted people we see in these pictures. Identifying and introducing them might be our special purpose on this day.

Isaiah 52:13—53:12

When Philip caught up with the chariot where the Ethiopian was riding and reading, this was the passage that sparked their conversation. The Ethiopian asked an excellent hermeneutical question: "About whom does the prophet say this, about himself or about someone else?" (Acts 8:34). And Philip responded by proclaiming to him the good news about Jesus (v. 35).

On this Good Friday, we will dispense with the scholarly musings about the possible subjects of this passage, and instead we will follow Philip in his understanding that this prophecy anticipates and describes Jesus Christ.

So many of the Old Testament prophesies that foresee a messianic figure and age are pictures of victory, prosperity, and an everlasting reign of peace by some son of David. This portrait of a tortured victim, an apparently helpless martyr, however, does not seem to square with those other, more potent images of the Messiah. Clearly Jesus' own disciples did not, at first, recognize and understand this part of what it meant for Jesus to be the Christ (see, for example, Mark 8:29-33).

The traditional hero defeats the enemy, and he rescues the innocent and the oppressed at the expense of their oppressor. But the hero of this prophecy is of a very different sort. Consider these against-the-grain statements: "He was wounded for our transgressions, crushed for our iniquities," "the Lord has laid on him the iniquity of us all," and he "made intercession for the transgressors." The people this hero rescues are not at all innocent. He does not rescue at the expense of some antagonist but at his own expense. This is the heroism of self-sacrifice and love.

The so-called suffering servant of this passage is revealed in terms of several relationships. There is a great fluidity in the author's use of personal pronouns, moving freely between first-, second-, and third-person references, both singular and plural, without any deliberate effort to identify the antecedents.

The insights to be discovered in an examination of these pronouns exceed the boundaries of this brief commentary. We could explore the relationships depicted between the servant and God, between the servant and us, between the servant and the unidentified "they" and "them" of the passage. As a starting point, however, I would recommend a careful look at just the first-person pronouns.

The first-person, singular pronouns, we presume, indicate that God is speaking. He is the one who would most naturally say things such as these: "See, my servant shall prosper," "[he was] stricken for the transgression of my people," and "I will allot him a portion with the great." The first-person, singular pronouns, therefore, give us a glimpse into the mind and purpose of God. And on this Good Friday, we may take the first-person, singular statements from this foreshadowing of the cross to explore what it was that God designed to accomplish on that day.

The first-person, plural pronouns, meanwhile, identify the statements that we can own. We may be the "we." One fruitful approach to this passage would be to look for ourselves in it. What part do we play on Good Friday? What is the suffering servant's relation to us, and what is our response to him? The old spiritual asks, "Were you there when they crucified my Lord?" And the first-person, plural pronouns of this suffering servant passage similarly invite us into the event.

Hebrews 10:16-25

When some authority figure walks into an existing situation — especially when that situation is a bit of a mess — and declares, "Now here's the way it's going to be from now on," it's usually a sign of a stricter regime. The fat will be cut. Discipline will be enforced. Heads will roll.

The writer of Hebrews, however, paints a very different picture of God's new regime. The situation is a mess, to be sure: a chronically sinful humanity, including a very disappointing chosen people. Yet, tellingly, when God declares the way it's going to be, it is not a message of martial law. Rather it's a message of love and grace.

Here is a great testimony to the heart of God and to a way in which he is so very different from us. He has not become fed up to the point where he has lost sight of his perfect picture. He has not been so discouraged or angered that he abandons his original plan. Instead, he declares how it's going to be, and the picture he paints is as gracious and perfect as it was at the start.

That God is willing — no, eager! — to make a new covenant, reveals his nature. He does not forfeit us to the sinfulness we have chosen. He does not lock the door behind the runaway child and say, "Good riddance!" Instead, he desires a new start with us, though we do not deserve it. And though we do not make very promising partners in this proposed arrangement, he is very promising.

He promises, first, to make a change within us. Rather than God's law remaining an external thing quite apart from us, he will make it an internal component — a part of us. He promises, second, to forgive our sins in this most remarkable way — a way that we human beings find nearly impossible to achieve in our relationships — he will "remember their sins... no more."

The writer of Hebrews is the great expositor of the gospel according to the Old Testament. After citing those Old Testament promises of God, he turns to the fulfillment of God's good purpose that is afforded us through Christ.

The statement that "we have confidence to enter the sanctuary by the blood of Jesus" will not make immediate sense to most of the people in our pews. Entering into the sanctuary, in our day, is about signage and accessibility. And confidence entering into the sanctuary is about user-friendliness and a welcoming atmosphere. Indeed, in so many churches, even the terminology of "sanctuary" has been abandoned.

Within the context that the writer of Hebrews has in mind, however, the sanctuary is the holy place. And who can enter there with confidence? Indeed, who can enter there at all?

The Old Testament design for regulations about the tabernacle all bear witness to a holy God. And human beings are not to wander casually in and out of the presence of this holy God. When the high priest made his prescribed annual entrance into the holy of holies, he took blood with him.

Now the writer of Hebrews assures us that we are all invited to enter the holy place and to approach the presence of God. We do so with confidence because of the blood by which we are saved, purified, and sanctified — that is, the blood of Jesus.

Indeed, Jesus dominates the entire scene as the writer reflects on that tabernacle and its rituals. Jesus is the new "great high priest." It is his blood by which we enter and it is through the curtain of his flesh that we approach the Father.

John 18:1—19:42

Customarily, we are given a paragraph or two as our gospel lection for an occasion. Not today. For this occasion, no excerpt will suffice. We need to see the whole scene and so we are presented with two entire chapters from John's gospel: his account of Jesus' crucifixion, all the way from Gethsemane on Thursday night to the garden tomb late Friday afternoon.

The gospel reports that Jesus went to a garden across the Kidron valley — a place Judas knew because Jesus had gone there often with his disciples. Here is one of so many pieces of evidence that Jesus was entering voluntarily into what was ahead for him. He knew what Judas was up to, and yet he did not take evasive action. Instead, he went to precisely the place where Judas would find him.

The image of Judas arriving with soldiers, police, and weapons is a preposterous one twice over.

At a human level, it is a massive case of overkill. Jesus had been within their reach day after day in the temple; yet they took no action against him. Did they think that he would resist? Did they think that there would be a great, violent resistance that would need to be overcome by force?

Meanwhile, at a supernatural level, this detachment is equally ridiculous, though in the other direction. While their show of force is laughably excessive, given Jesus' complete lack of resistance, it is embarrassingly paltry given Jesus' capacity. As he said in Matthew's account of the Gethsemane event, it would take just a word from him and the Father would dispatch twelve legions of angels to his aid (Matthew 26:53). How would the local soldiers and police have fared against that?

John's gospel does not give us the glimpse of tortured prayer that we find in other gospel accounts. Jesus is not facedown on a rock, sweating drops of blood, and praying that "this cup" be taken from him. Instead, Jesus stands tall in the face of his tormentors, in control of the entire situation, even though to all outward appearances he is the victim of jealousy, malevolence, and betrayal. He does not pray to have the cup taken from him but rather challenges the sword-flashing Simon Peter: "Am I not to drink the cup that the Father has given me?"

All four gospels record Peter's infamous denial of Jesus. John, however, may do the most artful job with the story, weaving it into the back-and-forth scene changes between Jesus' trial inside and Peter's pressure outside.

Meanwhile, the trajectory of Jesus' ordeal takes him from the garden to the house of the high priest. While Pilate's name is the notorious one, the high priest is the first to have a hand in the death of Jesus. His participation is a significant one, both in the tragic sense of God's own priest opposing his work and in the symbolic sense of the high priest's role in shedding blood to make atonement for the people.

From the high priest's house, Jesus was taken to the Roman governor, Pilate.

The picture of the Jewish leaders refusing to enter Pilate's headquarters in order "to avoid ritual defilement" is emblematic of the very kind of hypocrisy that Jesus so often criticized in them. Here, again, they strain the gnat but swallow the camel, for they are tiptoeing around ritual uncleanness, while running full-speed ahead into conspiracy, injustice, and opposition to God.

Of the four gospel writers, John gives us perhaps the fullest picture of Pilate. We see more of the content of his dialogue with Jesus, in addition to the familiar tug-of-war with the Jewish leaders and with the incited mob. We see here a man perceptive enough to recognize Jesus' innocence, secure enough that he did not seem personally threatened by Jesus or his kingdom claims, and ethical enough that he was not cavalier about the prospect of executing an innocent man. Yet it seems that he was not strong enough to resist being pushed into doing what he did not want to do.

Later, after the Jewish leaders object to the wording of the sign that Pilate had had posted above Jesus' head, he is intractable: "What I have written I have written." It seems, however, that this occasional virtue of not being pushed around, not catering to pressure from the locals in his jurisdiction, came too late.

Nicodemus, whom we met in the shadows of John 3, now reemerges on this grim occasion. He did not know, it seems, how to believe and follow Jesus when he was alive, but as Johnny-on-the-spot, he had to pay his respects to the dead. There may always be some who prefer a dead Lord. It is easier to bring our myrrh and aloes than it is to take up his cross and follow.

The burial of Jesus seems to have been a matter of expediency. "The tomb was nearby." That hasty entombment reminds us of just how quickly these events unfolded. On Thursday afternoon, the disciples were excitedly making preparations for a holiday meal together with Jesus. By Friday afternoon, he was dead. The whole thing was so sudden: his strange predictions at the supper table, the ambush in the garden, the mock trial, the quick sentencing, and then he was gone.

Application

As we weave together three passages — all very different, but which point to and depict the same event — we catch a glimpse of the assortment of people who were nearby.

First, perhaps at the greatest distance, see the antagonists. They are the conspiring Jewish leaders, the Roman governor, the mocking guards and torturing soldiers, and the bloodthirsty crowd. See their pictures in John's gospel as they carry out their wickedness against Jesus. Below those pictures, add the captions from Isaiah: "He was oppressed, and he was afflicted, yet he did not open his mouth." "By a perversion of justice he was taken away." "They made his grave with the wicked... although he had done no violence, and there was no deceit in his mouth."

Focus in more closely on that crowd of antagonists, and see there at the center the high priest. He, who was assigned by God to make atonement for the sins of the people, unknowingly prophesied that "it is better for you to have one man die for the people than to have the whole nation destroyed" (John 11:50). He is the one whose hand was so pivotal in shedding the blood of the once-for-all atoning sacrifice, unaware that his victim would become the new and eternal "great high priest over the house of God."

Now see the inner circle of people — the disciples, followers, and believers. They misunderstand. They run and hide. They deny. See their pictures in John's gospel and beneath their pictures add these captions from Isaiah's prophecy: "He was wounded for our transgressions, crushed for our iniquities; upon him was the punishment that made us whole, and by his bruises we are healed." "All we like sheep have gone astray; we have all turned to our own way, and the Lord has laid on him the iniquity of us all." "Who could have imagined his future?"

Then see the Father and the Son.

There is the Son, who set aside every human reflex in order to submit to the Father's plan so that "through him the will of the Lord shall prosper." And there is the Father, whose will it was "to crush him with pain," to "make his life an offering for sin," and then to "prolong his days." It was the Father "who laid on him the iniquity of us all," and the Father who "will allot him a portion with the great."

Last of all, there is us. We are in the picture because it is our iniquity, our wounds, and our transgressions. We are invited to be nearby, for by this event we are encouraged to "approach with a true heart in full assurance of faith."

An Alternative Application
John 18:1—19:42. "The One that Got Away." It is a natural human reflex to defend oneself. Something comes at your eye, and you blink. It's a natural, physical reflex.

Defending oneself is also the developed reflex of fear. Someone raises a hand to strike you, and you brace yourself. Perhaps you put your own arms up to protect; perhaps even to defend yourself by striking back.

Of course, it is also the unwholesome reflex of the ego to defend oneself too. If someone criticizes me, my instinct is to defend myself verbally. When I am at my worst, I respond by attacking verbally, as well. Someone misunderstands my actions or motives, and I am impatient to set the record straight. Someone finds fault with me, and I want to be able to answer with a reason or at least an excuse.

See how submissive to the Father's will Jesus was. He set aside the physical reflex, the fearful reaction, and the ego's instinct. Both the Isaiah prophecy and the gospel account bear witness to a man who made no natural effort to try to get away.

When he was being pursued, he did not run and hide. When he was surrounded, he did not lash out or resist. When he was accused, he did not defend himself. And when he was attacked and abused, he neither cursed nor cried for mercy, but prayed for the transgressors.

We have seen in other settings (like Luke 4:28-30 and John 8:58-59) that Jesus was able to get away from a physical threat. We have seen in earlier episodes (such as Matthew 21:23-27 and 22:15-22) that Jesus was able to extrude himself from verbal traps, as well. Who can fathom what supernatural aid he had at his disposal (see Matthew 26:52-53). Yet he made no effort to get away.

When it was all said and done, he did get away. He got away in a manner they could never have guessed. While he made no effort to get away from the betrayer, the accusers, the tormentors, or the executioners, on the third day he rose up and got away from the tomb!

Back to the garden

A first-time father glanced over at his wife as dawn began to break. Both were exhausted and had gone sleepless again because of their colicky newborn who cried the night away. "It must be time to get up," he told her, "the baby's finally asleep."

Sometimes it seems as if dawn will never come and the night will be an endless whimpering of pain and suffering. The metaphor is not only for those restless midnight-to-first-light watches but also for the fate of the human race. There is a darkness that surrounds us like oil and seeps through our societies with its vexing blight, filling news reports with violence, and back pages with obituaries. Night is with us always, and it is not our constant friend (see Psalm 88:18).

So it is a wonderful thing to remember on this Easter morning what Clement of Alexandria declared: "Jesus has turned all of our sunsets into sunrises." Similarly, when Houston Smith, the great scholar of religious studies at the University of California in Berkeley, pegged the seven major world religions to the clock (Confucianism at 9 a.m. for its social organizational motifs; Islam at noon when the brightness of the sun casts no shadow and all must bow in obedience; Taoism to the personal path that one begins to meander at 5 p.m. when the obligations of the work day are set aside; Buddhism to the supper hour of 7 p.m. and all the modest pleasures of simple life enjoyment; Judaism to sundown and rest as the reward of God's good favor; Hinduism to the midnight hour when all things merge into oneness), he taught that Christianity was the religion of the dawn. Christianity puts its face to the future and builds its hope from the passing of the dark night of sin into the promises announced by "That Great Gettin' Up Morning" relished in the old spiritual.

All of the gospels tie the importance of today to the garden tomb and the witness of its stark emptiness over against all other cemetery plots on this grave-littered planet. But John increases the impact by linking the garden of the tomb to the garden of Eden. In the most profound of reversals of fortune, according to the fourth gospel, the alienation that closed the garden of paradise at the beginning of our race's history is suddenly undone when Jesus reopens fellowship between God and humanity in the garden of Easter morning.

Peter's testimony to Cornelius resonates with the same historical condensation: a change in divine strategy emerges in the Easter garden and produces the dawning of the new age in which we live. Similarly, Paul's great instruction regarding death and resurrection to the Corinthian congregation is filled with echoes of dawn and morning and a return engagement between the Creator and the creature in the power of Easter's first fruits. Today, to paraphrase T.S. Elliot, we go back to the garden and know the place again for the first time.

Acts 10:34-43

Peter's short recital of salvation history is a gem of condensation and punch. Creation, Israel, Jesus, Pentecost, and the mission of the church are quickly packaged together and tied up with a call to believe.

But the words take on even more significance when understood within the development of the great ripples of grace that eddy outward through the book of Acts. Luke narrates the story of the early church along the pattern set by Jesus in 1:8 — "You shall receive power when the Holy Spirit comes on you and you shall be my witnesses in Jerusalem and in all Judea and Samaria, and to the ends of the world." He adds literary nuances that refine that global spread. Along with the big shift after chapter 12 that vaults Paul to the primary role of gospel presenter after the initial dozen chapters that focused on Peter, there is another, more subtle progression within the tale. The markings of this secondary advancement are noticed particularly in verses 6:7; 9:31; 12:24; 16:5; and 19:20. In each of these a similar refrain recurs. The "word of God" "grows" or "spreads" or "multiplies." These repetitious choruses mark the end of narrative sections in which a successive portion of society is penetrated and transformingly influenced by the message of Jesus and the resurrection. First, it is Jerusalem that revels in the good news (2:1— 6:7), then it is Judea and Samaria (6:8—9:31); later it will be Asia Minor (12:25—16:5) and Europe (16:6—19:20). But in between geographical advances comes the tale of a new harvest leaping beyond the Jewish world and landing feet-first in the kingdom of the Gentiles. 9:32—12:24 forms a section in which Peter becomes the bearer of the gospel across ethnic lines in the first deliberate missionary engagement of the kind.

It is striking to see that the message Peter brings to Cornelius, the Roman centurion stationed at Caesarea, is exactly the same as that announced to the Jews in Jerusalem on Pentecost Sunday. It is all about creation, Israel, Jesus, Pentecost, and the missionary message of the church. The critical junction in the story, as it is always told, is not the ethical wisdom of Jesus or even his healing miracles; rather it is his savage death and amazing resurrection. Easter is the heart of the gospel message. Everything changes because of Easter. When people struggled only to live for the hours of this lifetime they succeeded in various ways and attempted to make it through according to a variety of religious traditions. Now that Jesus has died and come back to life, the very playing field is altered. To make it through this life is not enough. We must also now face our Creator who judges both "the living and the dead" (v. 42). Therefore everyone, Gentile as well as Jew, is forced to deal in some way with Jesus. Religions, as well as life itself, can be favorable to Jesus or antagonistic to Jesus, but they cannot any longer ignore Jesus. Resurrection morning has revised the rules of the game.

Years ago, a newspaper editor assigned one reporter to write a human interest story about David Livingstone, the great pioneer missionary and explorer of Africa. The editor gave specific instructions: "Don't focus your attention on Livingstone's religion. Keep it about the man, the do-gooder, the humanitarian."

This was easier said than done, as the reporter found. For it is not possible to talk about Livingstone apart from his religion. There is no doing good without understanding the source of that good in Livingstone's perceptions. There is no humanitarian kindness apart from the kindness of God to humanity, which became the substance of Livingstone's testimony. Livingstone as a man is God's man. Even the epitaph written to commemorate him in Westminster Abbey subtly suggests the same by making allusions to 1 Peter 2:5: "He needs no epitaph to guard a name / Which men shall praise while worthy work is done. / He lived and died for good, be that his fame. / Let marble crumble; this is living stone."

So it is with Christianity. It can be evaluated on many fronts and understood through multitudinous dimensions. But at its heart, inseparable from any part of it as air is from life, is the resurrection of Jesus. Take that away and you no longer have Christianity. You may have an ethic or a sentiment or a philosophy or a moral code, but you will not have Christianity.

1 Corinthians 15:19-26

This is actually the second of Paul's letters to the Corinthian congregation from his third journey base of operations in Ephesus. Earlier he had sent a nasty scourge (see 5:9) that met with mixed response and resulted in a delegation coming to Paul for further clarification. It is clear to read this history in the language and themes of this letter. Chapters 1-3 address the problem of many competing groups within the congregation, and then tip over into Paul's need to defend his own authority in chapter 4. Paul was, after all, the source of the gospel message for the Corinthian church and the founder of its congregational character. Divisions in the church threatened to turn it into a balkanized amalgam where party politics undermined a unified sense of identity in Christ.

Paul goes on in chapters 5-6 to address the overt sinful behaviors that apparently had been the target of his earlier missal. One case involved a man shacking up with his father's wife in a manner that offended many in the congregation, and even more folks beyond, thus compromising any hope of effective witness about Jesus. The other incident was a public account of fellow church members suing one another in court and scandalizing the unity of the body of Christ. Paul's fingers wag menacingly as he warns the church to deal quickly and appropriately with these blights.

Then, beginning in chapter 7, Paul responds directly to the questions raised by members of the Corinthian congregation, seeking his wisdom and direction:

1. Should we encourage marriages or not (7:1-24)?
2. How should virgins handle their sexuality (7:25-40)?
3. Can we buy and eat the cheap meat in the markets that comes from pagan shrines and has been originally devoted to other gods (8:1—11:1)?
4. Are there any rules for appropriate worship services (11:2-16)?
5. Some are complaining about our Lord's Supper celebrations — what are we doing wrong (11:17-34)?
6. Which are the best spiritual gifts and how should they be used (12:1—14:40)?
7. What will happen to those in our community who have died (15:1-58)?
8. What's this collection you keep telling us about (16:1-4)?

Today's lectionary passage is the heart of Paul's response to the question about death in the early Corinthian congregation. While we enjoy the power of this passage as a strong literary treatise, we are often not aware of the intensity of both its original question or the power of Paul's answer. The idea of "resurrection" erupted as the core and central element of Christian preaching because of the uniqueness of Jesus' return to life on Easter. While there were religions and philosophies that speculated on the immortality of some spiritual inner essence of humankind, few shaped a doctrine of resurrection that was vitally gripping and described a full return to life of the full person. This is what made the message of Christianity stand out among the religions of its time.

Furthermore, there was a very strong sense in the preaching of the apostles that Jesus, who had recently returned to heaven, was about to come back to earth to finish the job of creation's restoration as the messianic age began. Jesus only went to heaven in order to allow time for the apostles to tell everyone about the events of his death and resurrection. Probably next week, or next month at the latest, the missionary blitz will be finished and Jesus will return.

There was a tremendous urgency about the witness of the church and the eschatological expectations of the believers generally. This made the recurring problem of deaths in the community a confusing challenge. Since Jesus was returning so soon, everybody expected to be there when he came, and a transition state for the dead was not even considered at first. But when Jesus delayed his parousia, and as more folks succumbed to illness or age, the cemetery pile-up became a problem. Hence the question of what happens to those who die before Jesus returns?

This question gives Paul the opportunity to restate the evidence of Jesus' resurrection and then go on to talk about the powerful change wrought by Easter. Death is our human lot. But Jesus shifts us into a parallel humanity, founded not only on the terminal resources of the first Adam, but on the eternal energies of the first fruits of the kingdom of God.

Death challenges us all, ever since it laid waste to the garden of Eden. But Jesus brings us back to the garden and offers us the antidote to the deadly virus that has ruled too long unchallenged. This time those who linger in the garden find life instead of death.

John 20:1-18

The two scenes in this lectionary passage are powerful in themselves, but take on extra significance when viewed within the framework of John's carefully crafted gospel presentation. First, John's commitment to reporting the details of events goes beyond merely stating the obvious. Already in the prologue to the gospel (1:1-18), two guiding principles become apparent — John is casting this story of Jesus as a deliberate corollary to the original creation account of Genesis 1, and "light" and "darkness" will therefore become key criteria by which to interpret what takes place.

Here these themes erupt into action. Jesus' resurrection takes place on "the first day of the week," both chronologically and symbolically. It is the calendar day of Sunday, as we call it. But it is also the theological day of creation when by divine fiat God dispels the chaotic darkness through the declaration that light shall overcome it. So John tells us that it is not only "early" on that first day of the week but that these things took place "while it was still dark." In other words, the gloom that had settled over planet earth as a shroud of sinful deception (see 1:1-18) still lingers, although God's new (re)creative work in Jesus is about to blast it away.

Second, when Mary looks into the empty tomb, she sees two angels at the place where Jesus' body had been laid. Here again, however, John adds important interpretive details. The two angels are not standing next to one another but are positioned at either end of the flat surface where Jesus' body had rested. Thinking back to chapter 1 we are reminded that when Jesus appeared, "We have seen his glory," according to John. This "glory" was one with that of the Father and is a clear reminder that when God appeared to God's people in Old Testament times, there was an expression of the *shekinah* glory that pervaded tabernacle and temple and took up residence on the mercy seat of the Ark of the Covenant. This mercy seat was the portable throne of Yahweh on earth and was guarded at either end by cherubim — angels who stood at attention. What John wishes for us to see as Mary looks into the tomb is that the "glory" of God as revealed in Jesus is no longer here, nor will it any longer be confined or localized to an earthly shrine. God has come to earth to create and re-create, bringing the light of heaven; now that work is accomplished, and we may live in the light wherever we go. And as John shows us next, follow that light eventually back into heaven itself.

Third, while Mary is weeping at the tomb, John reminds us that this all takes place in a garden. Furthermore, when Mary is approached by a man, she believes him to be the gardener. Why does John make a big deal of this? Because, in the early days of the original creation as recounted in Genesis, humans lived in a garden and the true "gardener" came to walk and talk with them there. After the divisive acts of sinful disobedience, the humans were thrust out of the garden and the days of intimate fellowship with the "gardener" were ended. Now, however, as re-creation begins to reshape life on planet earth, the "gardener" returns to the garden and pauses for conversation with those who too long have been alienated from him.

Fourth, this is confirmed in the fact that Mary is confused and doesn't understand anything until Jesus speaks her name. When Jesus says "Mary," everything suddenly falls into place. Mary knows who she is and begins to understand who Jesus is. Notice that John never denies or challenges the notion that this figure looming into Mary's sight range is the gardener. Instead, John allows that perception to stand but fills it with all its theological significance. As the true gardener speaks her name, Mary comes to life. Just as in the Genesis story where the Creator/gardener calls Adam by name and thus brings him into being.

Clearly, John is telling us of events that took place on the first Easter Sunday morning. Just as convincingly, John is calling our attention to those details that help us see the significance of all this as a renewing of the creation by the Creator who comes to restore light and life in a world that has been too long under the sway of darkness and death.

Application

Our cemeteries tend to look like gardens. Perhaps a play can be made on the idea of those who are entombed there as "Planted for Life." Of course, this planting is after the manner of Christian faith; not the irrevocable lostness of death without hope.

Dr. Alexander Simpson, who invented chloroform in his Edinburgh laboratory in 1847, was asked later in life what he considered his most valuable discovery. He astounded reporters by declaring that it was in finding the love of God. As testimony to this, when he and his wife buried their young daughter whose illnesses refused to be tamed even by her father's great skills, the gravestone contained only one word beside the typical name and dates: "Nevertheless..." It was Simpson's assurance that death had already been trumped by life.

An Alternative Application

John 20:1-18. While there is punch in the Acts reading and power in the epistle text, it is the gospel story that begs to be treated by itself this morning. Let Mary's experiences remind us of what Easter gives back to us: our friend Jesus, our very selves, and the lives of our loved ones lost during the years past.

Witness: suffering and rejoicing with hope

Is the church living post-Christendom or post-Easter? Are Christians today discouraged by the world in which they live? Or are Christians excited by the world in which they live? It is said that perception is everything. While this is a business/public relations/advertising mantra that caters to the subjective, it may be useful for a moment to make a point.

How do Christians perceive the world in which they believe and witness? As we take our cues from the New Testament, we must concede that we live as a post-Easter people, which should excite us to the third heaven (as it did an acquaintance of Paul). Whatever we want to say about our post-Christendom world (i.e., the church can no longer be taken for granted as the cultural center of our society, nor can we expect the society in general to reflect the particular Christian ethos), this is only the context in which we witness. It is not the formative ground from which we view the world. The formative ground on which we stand and from which we view the world is located just outside the empty tomb down the road from Calvary.

In a sense, we should neither decry nor applaud the fact that we live *in* a post-Christendom context. For, in truth, we *live* post-Easter! This perception is everything! It shapes the witness of the believer, who suffers the misperceptions of a sinful world while rejoicing in the marvelous manifestations of the love of God through Jesus' life, passion, crucifixion, and resurrection.

Acts 5:27-32

The apostolic church had a disciplined witness. It was disciplined in giving, in sharing, and in suffering. To appreciate more fully the latter, it would be helpful to be reminded of the former. For this we will need to review a couple passages prior to this account of imprisonment of the apostles.

One of the striking characteristics of the apostolic church that Luke lifts up is the sharing of resources among the believers, such that "there was not a needy person among them" (Acts 4:34). In principle, this first congregation "had everything in common" (Acts 4:32). In a very practical way, their experience with Jesus placed them all on the same playing field. It is in light of this that the disposition of one's personal possessions was so important (see also Acts 2:43-47).

Enter Ananias and Sapphira (Acts 5:1-11). Their story is told in sharp contrast to the spirit of the congregation. The consequences of their actions are most sobering. It would not stretch the imagination too far to see a parallel here with the first covenant people of God. When they murmured against God's ways in the wilderness, they too were judged. Ananias and Sapphira were not content with how the Spirit of God was organizing the apostolic church in terms of its shared generosity. Wanting to keep more for themselves, they conspired to rebel against the work of God. Like the people in the wilderness who were judged by earthquake (Numbers 16:1-40; Korah's rebellion) or by snake bite (Numbers 21:4-9; murmurings in the wilderness), this anti-stewardship couple was judged in a most dramatic fashion.

Is it any wonder that the apostles were so bold in their witness, even in the face of imprisonment? When they experienced the power of the Spirit of God bonding them together in common through generous sharing of resources, caring for each other's needs, and miracles of healing for "the sick and those afflicted with unclean spirits" (Acts 5:16), they were made all the more confident in their defense of the faith before the religious authorities. "We must obey God rather than men" (5:29).

This present imprisonment is not the first time Peter and John had been arrested and placed in custody. Nor would it be their last. Yet, this did not deter them. As Peter explained, what God had done through Jesus in raising him from the dead and in providing forgiveness of sins was far too important and powerful to be suppressed by human fears or jealousies. Peter ends his response with a reference to obedience (5:32). The role of the witness is to give testimony dutifully. Peter and the other apostles had been privileged to see and hear Jesus, before his crucifixion and after his resurrection. They were privy to the most intimate revelation of God in the world from the beginning of time. There was no way they would shirk their responsibility to testify to the one who was "leader and Savior" (5:31).

Jesus, as leader into resurrection life (Acts 3:15), would be made perfect through his suffering (Hebrews 2:10). Those who would be obedient to him should expect no less a life of suffering from the same world that rejected him.

After Gamaliel counsels caution to the council (Acts 5:33-39), the disciples are beaten in chastisement (a foretaste of suffering still to come!) and admonished not to speak in the name of Jesus again. In a response that only those who are thoroughly convinced of the truth can understand, the apostles rejoice in their sufferings (Acts 5:41; see also, Romans 5:3-5 and 2 Corinthians 4:7-12), as they continue to proclaim the name of Jesus.

Revelation 1:4-8

It is very likely that this visionary book was written during the reign of Domitian (81-96 AD). As emperor, he took emperor worship very seriously, calling himself "savior" and "lord" and having statues erected all over the empire, not just in his honor, but also for his worship. This put the Christian believer in dire straights. For there was "no other name under heaven given among men by which we must be saved" (Acts 3:12). What were Christians to do when confronted with the choice of worshiping Caesar and prospering as a good citizen of Rome or of worshiping only God through Jesus and not bowing down to Caesar and therefore risk losing freedom, home, employment, family, and life itself?

When the churches in Asia Minor were confronted with this situation, John stepped forward and shared his vision in order that the church may be guided by the one true light and not be misguided into the dark alleys of fear, doubt, and disbelief. From the *get-go*, John reminds his readers that Jesus is "the ruler of kings on earth" (1:5). Caesar may seem to be all-powerful and everywhere present throughout the empire, but it is God who is the beginning and end of life itself (the alpha and omega — the first and last letters of the Greek alphabet). This is Jesus, crucified and now risen. His resurrection is a singular event. He is the "first-born from the dead" (1:5). To follow and obey him will get the believer farther down the road of life than conceding anything to Caesar, even if suffering is part of the journey. To be faithful witnesses to the one who is called "the faithful witness" (1:5) would be the greatest honor, even if martyrdom would result. Seeing how God the Father rewarded Jesus' faithfulness sends an encouraging message to those who would strive to be faithful even unto death. In truth, Jesus promises "the crown of life" (Revelation 2:10; how ironic that the first Christian martyr was named Stephen, whose name means "crown") to those who are so obedient. Paul would argue in his letter to the Romans, "If we have been united with him in a death like his, we shall certainly be united with him in a resurrection like his" (Romans 6:5).

With this confidence, the Christian can feel safe even in the midst of persecution, like books being held in place by bookends, like all the letters of the alphabet contained between the first and the last. God brackets our lives, such that there is nothing outside the grasp of God. Come what may, the believer is God's! Though the devil may have his day, God will have his way! This is the spiritual truth that gives the believer strength and comfort in trying times.

John 20:19-31

The gospel writer John is really the kindest to his readers in terms of the ending of his account of Jesus' life. Matthew, true to his teaching purposes, leaves the reader in the middle of a conversation. Jesus gives the Great Commission to his disciples; then, period. No further comments, no response from the disciples, no resolve as to where Jesus goes from here. Luke is a bit more gracious on this matter; he includes the ascension and reports that the disciples rejoiced by worshiping God daily. Mark messes with our minds and leaves the point of his sermon a mystery! "Figure it out for yourselves," he seems to say. "I'm just going to leave you hanging with the disciples who were totally discombobulated by the events that occurred." Those who were unhappy with Mark's seeming lack of closure added another softer ending that combines what Luke and Matthew did (Mark 16:9-20). John is extremely reader-friendly in his closing. He tells us exactly why he wrote the gospel (20:30-31). The epilogue is like the denouement after the climax in a novel and simply trails off with a personal authentication of the testimony and an offhand remark about how much Jesus really did beyond the scope of the gospel record.

Jesus' appearance to the ten apostles on Easter evening has the purpose of comforting and settling them with the truth of his resurrection and then giving them a commission. "Peace be with you. As the Father has sent me, even so I send you" (20:21). What Matthew does with a well-structured Great Commission (Matthew 28:13-20; statement of authority, purpose of the commission, method of discipling, and assurance), John expresses with a modeling metaphor. Just as Jesus was sent by the Father to the world, so the disciples are sent by Jesus into the world. With the Holy Spirit, they are empowered to forgive sins or to retain sins. Remembering the synoptic story of the healed paralytic (Matthew 9:1-8; Mark 2:1-12; Luke 5:17-26), this was tantamount to giving the disciples the voice of God in the course of human discourse: Blasphemy to some but a treasure in earthen vessels for others.

Because it was considered blasphemy by the religious leaders of the Jews, the disciples had cause to fear them. It was prudent for them to be behind closed doors. Fortunately, Jesus knew where to find his timid band of followers. He knew what they needed. When Thomas finally encountered the risen Jesus, he acknowledged him, "My Lord and my God!" (20:38). One can almost hear the confidence echoing through the centuries to us today. It certainly resounded in the streets, courts, and prisons of that day. Those who had been behind shut doors, once they witnessed Jesus risen from the dead, set their fears aside and boldly witnessed to him, despite what consequences lay in store. The same apostles who were huddled together on the first day of the week were on the streets, at Solomon's portico, and in the temple proclaiming the name of Jesus as Messiah for all the morrows of their lives.

Application

More and more the Western church is awakening to the persecutions against the body of Christ that have and are taking place around the world. The resurrection may have glorified Jesus' body, but his church is still suffering the crucifixion in many corners of the world. From the Middle East to China to Sudan, the news reports malicious actions taken by those in power against Christian minorities. What disciplines can be entered into by those who wish to make a difference for peace and justice on behalf of sisters and brothers in Christ?

In the spirit of Peter who stood before the authorities on behalf of the gospel and the apostolic community, we can discipline ourselves to prayer (Acts 2:42). Like a seatbelt, we can fasten our spiritual brothers and sisters to God with our prayers. Prayer can also arouse our own spirits to become involved in the answer to our prayers. Material support can be provided by the wealthy Western congregations for those who have less and are more vulnerable to the oppression of local authorities. Congregations can be inspired to reach out in physical ways to provide what is lacking in other fellowships that are enduring persecution. Moral and political support can also be garnered through education and advocacy on behalf to those whose voice is muffled by sobs and tears. For example, Amnesty International (www.amnestyusa.

org) and Voice of America (www.voanews.com) provide avenues for education and advocacy. In our age of communication, ignorance is no longer an excuse. Neither is inconvenience, since we can access so much and reach out so far from the comfort of our own home computer.

Suffering does not just come at the hands of those who persecute Christians. There are many other sources of suffering in the Christian's daily life: bad health (physical and mental), work stress, job loss, broken relationships, criminal decisions, accidents, intrusive and abusive people, self-doubts. Congregations also can suffer as a body from complainers and dissenters, poor leadership (lay and clergy), demographic and economic changes in the neighborhood, strategic deaths or transfers of key people, catastrophic weather that destroys the facility or kills many members. Yet, in the midst of all these possibilities, Jesus stands with us and for us, championing our cause with a tenacity that will not be thwarted by "things present, nor things to come" (Romans 8:38). Having this knowledge, believing this to be true is what gives the disciple of any age in any age "the peace of God, which passes all understanding" (Philippians 4:7). It even allows the disciple the strange response of rejoicing in the midst of suffering or shortly thereafter, as the Psalmist writes, "Weeping may tarry for the night, but joy comes with the morning" (Psalm 30:5).

In the spirit of *Shema* (Deuteronomy 6:4-9), Christians are to carry with them the confession of Jesus — in the words of no-longer-doubting Thomas, "My Lord and my God!" However, in our age of conciliation and compromise, we often capitulate the heart of our creed for the sake of better human relationships and at the sake of the truth. We become overwhelmed by a new age homogeneity that filters out distinctions and contradictions to reduce truth to what we can hold in common.

Here are some of the ways this is expressed in the general public square: "Well, whatever you believe that gets you by, that's what's important." Or, "I don't care what you believe as long as you believe in something." Or, "We're all going to the same place; it's just that some of us get there by a different route." Or, "There's only one God who loves us as we are, so it's okay that we understand God in our own way that makes sense to us." Or, "We're really not all that different; anyway, who's to say just who is right or wrong about this or that?"

These statements reflect our neopagan culture, which has moved beyond the Christendom of the West since the fourth-century AD to the close of the last century. "We're not in Kansas anymore, Toto!" More than ever before, Christians need to be clear about their faith: Jesus alone is the Messiah through whom alone is life that is eternal. John had no doubts about this and made it clear in his gospel. Christians today need to have this clarity of John and the boldness of Peter in professing the faith publicly so that others may believe and find the life in his name.

A complacent Western church must listen to the witness of the third-world Christians and also Christians who are suffering persecutions in so many lands around the globe. They understand what it means to witness to the truth, especially in the face of suffering. Yet, because they believe Jesus to be the Christ, the Son of God, risen from the dead, they also experience the joy that comes fresh every morning, like the songbird in the tree at sunrise.

The hope of the believer is that no person is so lost or no society is so dead that the love of God through Jesus cannot rise to reveal sin that can be forgiven, grief that can be comforted, fear that can be overcome, anxiety that can be relieved, evil that can be transformed. Such hope is possible for anyone who will dare to put one's finger into the wounds of Jesus, whose sacrificial death was requited on that sacred Sunday morning.

Finding ourselves in being found in Jesus

Socrates' famous dictum, "Know thyself," has been passed down through the ages in philosophy classes and psychology classes as instructors and students struggle with the perennial human question, "Who am I?" A couple of the fundamental keys we have in answering that question are family, name, friends, and work. Our first experience in identity is reflected through our up-bringing. We learn who we are by the intimate circle of people around us at the kitchen table, in the bathroom, and under the covers. As we learn our name, it becomes a most important handle with which to get a hold of ourselves; though what it says about our identity other than a label by which others call us, we are hard pressed to say — until we get into the meaning of names and hope the origin and signification of our name at least catches our fancy. When we are old enough to form a cadre of friends, we begin to learn so much about ourselves, as we play our thoughts, emotions, and behaviors against these others who have come into our lives like walking mirrors. Then, too, how we express ourselves through our work becomes an identifier for who we understand ourselves to be, although this is fraught with the dangers of relying too much on external factors to come to grips with an intensely internal personal dynamic.

The Bible directs us to "know the Lord" (see Jeremiah 31:34) and promises us that, as we do, we will know ourselves and ultimately learn the deepest meaning to our lives. This was Paul's experience. He learned his true identity only after his encounter with the risen Jesus. Not only do we learn who we are when we "consider Jesus" (Hebrews 3:1), we also discover what we are to do with our lives. Peter found this out after he ate breakfast with the risen Jesus.

One's fingerprints, Social Security number, driver's license, iris scan, or DNA test will reveal something about identity — who am I? But, it is only in one's encounter with the risen Jesus that we understand the meaning of this who that I am and the *what* that I am to do with my life.

Acts 9:1-6 (7-20)

When we first meet Paul, Luke refers to him in his Hebrew nomenclature and describes him as young and consenting to Stephen's death (Acts 7:58; 8:1). Acting as a kind of "coat check," he has so much to learn! At the time, he thinks he has a good idea of who he is. His later comments about his pedigree (Philippians 3:4-6) confirm a rather high opinion of himself. With his identity *intact*, he proceeds on his mission in life — to eradicate the sect of the way. Saul ravages the Christian church (Acts 8:3, imperfect tense indicating a continuing act of destruction and ruination, such that one translator, not erroneously, put deliberate intent into the sense of Saul's actions: "Saul *attempted to destroy* the church").

Our text begins with a more poetic, though not necessarily euphemistic, description of Saul's activity. He is described as "breathing heavily" (9:1) against the faithful in terms of threats (Acts 26:11) and actually following through on his threats (Acts 26:10). Saul is acting with zeal. He has a passion, fueled with a deep sense as to who he himself is. Perhaps the depth of his passion for persecution is revealed reflectively in his converse passion for proclaiming the faith at great risk to himself and also great pain (see 2 Corinthians 11:21b-29). The murderer of the faithful becomes a missionary to and for the faithful, regardless of the cost to himself. This is a radical turn around that is occasioned by his meeting the risen Jesus. How fascinating it would be to know more of the anecdotal moments of Christian encounter and internal dialog that preceded this monumental event and laid the seed for such a fruitful development in his story!

It is interesting to note that on the road to Damascus there is no condemnation of Saul by Jesus. He simply identifies himself and gives instructions for Saul. Reminiscent of Samuel in the temple, Saul responds by doing what is required of him. He goes into Damascus and waits for Ananias to restore his sight. Ananias, reminiscent of Moses' hesitancy to go into the court of Pharaoh, follows the instructions of his vision. Saul's sight is restored after three days. In preparation, Saul had undergone a complete fast (three days) and had sat in darkness. It is only in his own darkness that Saul will finally see the true light, as John writes, "The light shines in the darkness and the darkness has not overcome it" (John 1:5).

When all is said and done, Saul receives three visions. The first is the one of the risen Jesus on the road to Damascus. The second is about Ananias coming in to call on him. The third is when the scales fall from his eyes and he sees that Jesus is indeed the Christ, "the Son of God" (Acts 9:20, 22). God's work with Saul has been complete and thorough. These visions changed Saul. The first encouraged him to continue to his original destination but with a different agenda now. The second prepared him to be beholding to a disciple of the way, giving him a different paradigm with which to view these previous objects of his scorn. This would be the beginning of a new love in Saul's heart that would find expression in such letters as Philippians, Thessalonians, Timothy, and Philemon. The third led him into a new career. He was baptized and began preaching the name of Jesus, rather than persecuting the name of Jesus.

We can only begin to imagine the consternation of the Jews. They thought they knew and understood Saul. His reputation had preceded him. But, identities have a way of changing to their true character when the risen Jesus is involved. Saul came to know himself so much better, so much fuller, and so much deeper after he met the risen Jesus on the road to Damascus. His life took on a new trajectory, as he was inspired by seeing Jesus for who he truly is — the crucified and risen one. In light of this, he discovered himself, who he had been and who he was destined to be (1 Corinthians 15:9-11).

Revelation 5:11-14

These few verses are the concluding descriptor of the heavenly worship that is reported in chapters 4 and 5 of Revelation. After introducing himself as the seer and Jesus as the seen in chapter 1, and after sounding the seven messages to the seven churches (No batch email here! Each a personal word!), John is transported to the heavenly throne room through an open door. *Worship should always be an open door through which the glory of God is manifest!*

God is seated on the throne, surrounded by majestic color. Surrounding the throne are 24 thrones on which the elders are seated. There are also four sleepless, living creatures, who "never cease to sing, 'Holy, holy, holy, is the Lord God Almighty' " (Revelation 4:8). The 24 elders take their cues from them and join in a heavenly chorus of praise. Looking carefully, one can see a lamb in the midst of this wonderful scene — at once slain, yet very much alive and worthy to take the judgment scroll from the hand of God. The praise of the elders turns now to the lamb, whose exploits on earth are rehearsed with a melody from Calvary (Revelation 5:9).

This is the context in which the angels appear and join the song of praise to the lamb, who continues to be the center of attention in this sound-bite of heavenly worship. To the lamb is ascribed a plentitude of benediction: to the lamb belong power, wealth, wisdom, might, honor, glory, and blessing. There is a mouthful! No wonder it took "myriads of myriads and thousands of thousands" to get it all expressed! Even the creatures of earth chime in with concurring verse.

There is a totality of worship pictured here. Heaven and earth resound with it. The creatures from above and below cannot keep silent. At the heart of the worship, coursing with truth and life-giving joy, is the acknowledgment of Jesus, who is worthy of such adoration because of his work on the cross. He was slain and his blood was shed (like the sacrificial lambs of Old Testament times), so that a people could be ransomed from sin and death, given identity as citizens of God (kingdom) and purpose to serve God (priests). See Revelation 5:10.

With such a vision of heaven and earth united in adoration of Jesus, the worshiper can withstand the judgment of God, which will be unleashed from his hands as he breaks open the seals on the scroll. Thank God that the judgment scroll is held by such hands, for it was those same hands that were pierced out of mercy for the fallen! Not unlike Job, then, the believer will hold fast in faith, even when threatened to be trampled under the thundering hooves of the four horsemen and all that is to follow.

John 21:1-19

The post-resurrection appearances of Jesus are important in the gospel account to verify the nature of the resurrection itself. The mere physicality of the descriptions is a blatant clue informing the reader how to perceive this portion of the narrative. Rather than psychologizing or mythologizing the resurrection, John takes care to construct the story with tangible elements, so as to convince the reader/would-be believer that Jesus truly overcame death bodily. Indeed, Paul talks about a dramatic new creation in Christ (2 Corinthians 5:17; see also Romans 6:5 and Hebrews 10:20). His claims for new life are grounded in the radical nature of the resurrection.

Like a second ending to revisit this phenomenal event before letting it go with the final stroke of the pen, John reports the seaside experience. Previous to the fishing and breakfast escapade on the beach, Jesus had appeared to Mary Magdalene by the tomb and to the disciples twice in Jerusalem (John 20). Now, seven of the disciples have a spicy encounter with Jesus, seasoned with angling advice, a shared breakfast, and conversation about demonstrating love.

We find the disciples no longer huddled together behind closed doors for fear but rather out and about under the sun, moon, and stars. Maybe they were trying to get back into the routine of their lives before their three years with Jesus. Maybe they were simply hungry. Maybe they were still waiting around for guidance as to what to do with all that they had experienced — like John's version of a Pentecost event. Men do not wait well, so they get busy doing what they do best — before football, baseball, basketball, and racquetball were invented. They go fishing!

It is curious that in the boat at 100 yards off shore, the disciple John could identify the man on the beach as Jesus. It was not that his eyesight was better than 20/20. He was able to read the signs. The catch of fish upon his instruction pointed to the man as Jesus himself. Of course, Peter was all too ready to believe that. Remember, he had seen Jesus in the closed room twice already. So, he eagerly and whimsically threw himself into the sea to arrive first on the shore to greet Jesus. The others came in their laden boat. Who knows what the purpose is for mentioning that exactly 153 fish were caught, other than being a simple way of underscoring the record, the material content of all who are involved, the risen Jesus included. He is, after all, the one who invited the disciples to prepare their fish on a fire that he apparently had already started.

Perhaps at a distance it is easier to believe things. One can simply make up one's mind just what is to be imagined and accepted and then simply assert that it is so; offer a few proofs and not worry too much about the details. Hence, the confidence at 100 yards. But, when eye-to-eye in the very matrix of the stuff of life, it is harder to come to claims other than the material description of what simply is verifiable in a scientific, pragmatic way. Hence, the odd comment that once on shore, shoulder to shoulder with Jesus "none of the disciples dared ask him, 'Who are you?' " (21:12). As if they had some doubt somewhere in the recesses of their common sense brains; really, now, when was the last time the Romans let a condemned, crucified individual who had been placed in a sealed tomb slip through their hands?

However, in the shared meal (just like with the disciples who were on their way to Emmaus), Jesus is revealed as risen. The meal becomes the occasion for the disciples to have their eyes opened wider to the grand reality of the resurrection of the crucified one. John does not hesitate to tag this as "the third time

Jesus was revealed to the disciples after he was raised from the dead" (21:14).

Having been so identified, Jesus turns to Peter for a lesson in consequences. If he loves Jesus, then he will serve his bidding. Once we have clear who Jesus is, our identity is also shaped and our purpose is exposed. We are "fishers of men" or followers of Jesus or disciples or Christians or believers in the way. The descriptors are many. The point is that our identity is locked up in his identity. This is why the New Testament writers so often exhort the Christian to imitate Christ, live worthy of the gospel, do as Jesus would do, be an ambassador for him, and find gain in him. This being the case, our purpose becomes clear. We are to serve him. This is expressed by Jesus' threefold questioning of Peter about his love. If he loves Jesus, then he will feed his sheep. This is a metaphor for caring for the church, the believers, any who would claim Jesus as Lord and Savior and those who need to claim him as Lord and Savior.

It would be hard to miss the parallel here from the foot washing lesson in the upper room on the Thursday before his trial. He clearly said that he gave them an example to follow. Foot washing is a sign of servanthood, which is the quality that best characterizes the followers of Jesus. They are to be servants one of another, as well as servants to the needs of all of God's hurting creation. Now, on the beach, the lesson is the same, although it comes through the aroma and flavor of grilled fish. Just as Jesus provided his disciples with breakfast, so too are they to provide for the needs of others in any and all ways through which the love of God may shine and be manifest in tangible ways.

Application

The two most defining questions for humans to answer are *Who am I?* and *What am I to do?* Christians find the answers to these questions in the encounter with Jesus, crucified and risen. Just as Saul was confronted with himself when he met the Lord on the road to Damascus, so are we exposed to the presence of the one who is "the image of the invisible God" (Colossians 1:15). Pursued by the risen Jesus, Saul discovered himself to be the very one who was persecuting the Savior of the world, as he attacked his body, the church, in the world.

Fortunately, Jesus had other plans for Saul and led him in a new way, so that he himself could be a proclaimer of the way. Saul would be known to the world as Paul, the author of such identity quotes as "Wretched man that I am. Who will deliver me from this body of death? Thanks be to God through Jesus Christ our Lord" (Romans 7:24) and "Whether we live or whether we die, we are the Lord's" (Romans 14:8b). He also had a clear sense of his purpose, as expressed in 2 Corinthians 5:20, "We are ambassadors for Christ, God making his appeal through us." Also, "Of this gospel I was made a minister... to preach to the Gentiles the unsearchable riches of Christ" (Ephesians 3:7-8).

With these two fundamental questions answered, the where and the how of life are secondarily important. It is telling to observe that Saul continued on his way to Damascus. In a similar way, Christians today should keep alert to where they are actually living and working, rather than dream about far off places or even flock to different locales than the one God has already put them in. God did not change Saul's geography radically that day. He simply led Saul to do things radically different in the very place he was going, because of his encounter with the risen Savior. So, too, Christians today need to discover how to see the mission field in their own backyard. This is especially true as our nation moves deeper into being a post-Christian society with post-modern sensitivities that make us a field ripe unto harvest.

One of the great challenges the church faces today is proclaiming the relevance of Jesus in a relative world. Deconstructionist temptations abound to sap the essence out of the gospel. The unique, final, universal, efficacious, and sufficient quality of Jesus' life, death, and resurrection stand over against all tendencies to relegate him to the ranks of the many prophets who populate history, or to recognize him as important only insofar as the Christian community mythologizes his story toward parochial and selective ends pertinent but to its own perspective, or to judge him simply as a misguided religionist in what would be better as a religionless world. The hymn of Revelation echoes the sense of what C.S. Lewis meant when he wrote in *Mere Christianity* that Jesus either was who he said he was, namely the Son of God, or he is no better off than a man who thinks of himself as a poached egg — or worse, he is the very devil from hell!

There is a T-shirt with this written on it: "Hey, Doood! If you are going to take up space on this congested li'l planet, then shouldn't you at least have a point?!" As Peter learned his point to "Feed my sheep," we learn that we are to serve the Lord in ways that make use of our talents, interests, opportunities, and resources. Then our lives have a point! Faith in Jesus is acted out in tangible, practical ways that serve our neighbor by proclaiming the gospel of Jesus clearly and boldly and by caring for the many needs of the neighbor. In this way we are the voice, hands, and feet of our Lord in the world today — an expression and extension of his resurrected body.

Easter 4
Acts 9:36-43
Revelation 7:9-17
John 10:22-30
Mark Molldrem

How can the dead testify?

We have an affair with death that ranges from fascination to revulsion. Consider the telling analysis of Jessica Mitford's *The American Way of Death Revisited* (which first came out in 1963 and was updated in 1998), the psychological plumbing of Elizabeth Kübler-Ross' *On Death and Dying*, the emergent attentiveness in the West to *The Tibetan Book of the Dead*. Perhaps Woody Allen captured the pop cultural attitude best when he said, "I do not want to attain immortality through my work; I want to attain it by not dying."

The season of Easter gives us pause to reflect upon the universal destiny of life as we know it — death — juxtaposed to the proffered reality of new life in Jesus Christ not only for earthly time but also for eternal existence. Tabitha, Peter, John, white-robed martyrs, and angels give us something to ponder as we hear Jesus say about the sheep who hear the good shepherd's voice and follow, "I give them eternal life, and they shall never perish" (John 10:28).

Acts 9:36-43

Tabitha was a good Christian woman, "full of good works and acts of charity" (9:36). Yet, she got sick and died. In a religious worldview that saw things in a balance, there must have been many questions raised. Evil is to be punished and good is to be rewarded. This is the balance that makes sense with a moral God at the helm of the universe. Psalm 1 testifies to it. Job's friends argue for it. We can only speculate as to the kinds of questions that may have raced through the minds of her Christian friends, as to why such a good Christian woman would be afflicted so and the Christian community hurt by her loss.

One thing we know for sure is that they sent for Peter, presumably for his pastoral presence and comfort in their time of grief. Or, could they have been looking for something else, something more dynamic, something explosive? After all, Peter had been in neighboring Lydda where he had healed Aeneas, a man bedridden for eight years with paralysis (Acts 9:32-35). Perhaps he could do something miraculous on behalf of Tabitha. Had not his Master — and hers — raised Lazarus from the dead? Did not the Master say that they would do signs even more wonderful than that (John 5:12-14)? Death is an unwelcome guest — or should one say intruder? What lengths will one go to repel the thief that steals the precious gift of life from God?

When Peter comes, he finds no fleet-footed gazelle, but a death-bagged trophy ready for mounting on the wall of the slain. This does not deter him. In prayer, he faces death itself, like Ursula LeGuin's Festin in *The Word of Unbinding*, and counters its powers with a command from a new day: "Rise!" Unable to withstand, death cowers and releases its prey. The gazelle is afoot again.

Earlier in Acts Peter proclaims the name in which he performs such a sign of God's powerful presence in the world: "In the name of Jesus Christ of Nazareth" (Acts 3:6). This invocation was pronounced over a lame man, who responds by walking. It may be that to avoid any appearance of magical incantations, the disciples, like Peter, are not always cited with a formula response to people in need. Each situation of God's signature seems to have its own character and depends on the act itself to testify to the living presence of Jesus, rather than a pre-set order of chosen words or even ritual actions.

Worthy of note is the role the miracles play in the narrative. They serve as vehicles to convey people from the spectator curb into the flow of traffic that turns to the Lord, believes in the Lord, and moves to the destination of faith. The residents of Lydda were transported in this way; so, too, were the residents of Joppa (Acts 9:35, 42). Notice also that their belief was not "in Peter," but "in the Lord." Peter was but the instrument the risen Lord used to extend his will into the life of Tabitha and the witnesses of such deeds.

Revelation 7:9-17

Just before the seventh seal becomes the seven trumpets, breaking an interlude of heavenly silence, there is a brief conversation between the seer of Revelation and one of the elders. The topic of conversation is a great multitude, "standing before the throne of God and before the lamb" (7:9). They are the witnesses from "the great tribulation" (7:14), which was most likely the persecution of Christians under the reign of Domitian in the later part of the first century.

Domitian was big into emperor worship, referring to himself as "savior," "lord," and "god." Despite the egomania involved in such claims, the practice of emperor worship served a political function of unifying the empire under the symbol of Caesar, while allowing the worship of any other number of regional gods in addition. Yet, the Christians owed their primary allegiance to God, before whom there could be no other in heart or in stone. For refusing to take the oath of allegiance to Caesar and rendering the required offering at his image, the Christians were persecuted even unto death. Whether this persecution was throughout the entire empire or regionally focused in Asia Minor is not entirely clear. What seems to be evident is that the book of Revelation is addressed specifically to the churches in southwest Asia Minor for whom the persecution was real.

The multitude gathered is an innumerable, inclusive lot. There are no human boundaries that can exclude one from belonging to the faithful (7:9). This band of believers stands, palms in hand, with ready praise to God, like the crowd on Palm Sunday greeted Jesus as he entered Jerusalem. They acclaim, despite their tribulation, that salvation (not just in a psychological "wholeness" sense or a physical "well-being" sense, but in the eschatological sense of God's ultimate, inevitable, effective, and final victory over evil and death itself) belongs to God, the one who indeed reigns above and over and beyond anything Caesar can imagine. To this the angels agree with a resounding "Amen," while affirming the multitude's acclaim, launches them into a refrain of their own, ascribing wondrous attributes to God "for ever and ever" (literally, "into the ages of ages"). In this brief sound-bite, we hear those from heaven and those from earth join together in antiphonal chorus. The multitude has passed through death to life to join in celestial hymnody. Their witness cannot be silenced by any act of Caesar; from on high their testimony will resound to encourage those still below to be faithful.

As is true with so much of the book of Revelation, there is reliance on Old Testament texts for the substance of message as well as the imagery of expression. For example, the hymn "Salvation belongs to our God" (7:10) can be seen as a direct quote of Psalm 3:8. Isaiah 4:5-6 provides vivid imagery of God's sheltering presence, which Revelation 7:15 evokes. Who could read Revelation 7:16-17 and not hear an echo of Isaiah 25:8 and 49:10? What the Old Testament expressed in timely yet timeless words, the New Testament sets forth as fulfilled in the revelation of Jesus Christ, who has come and will come — the lamb, whose blood has been shed in time and for all time.

John 10:22-30

How can the dead testify? Taking the gospel of John as a sermon on faith in Jesus, crucified and risen, we can hear Jesus tell the Jews who were questioning him that indeed he will testify to his identity even from the grave. "The works that I do in my Father's name, they bear witness to me" (10:25). His greatest work was to die for the sins of the people and effect atonement with God. "As Moses lifted up the serpent in the wilderness, so must the Son of Man be lifted up, that whoever believes in him may have eternal life"

(John 3:15). From the grave, he would cry out to the world (through the preached word!), "See how much I love you? See to what length I will go to have you back where you belong? I will go into your darkest corner, death itself, to assure you that there is nowhere that my hand cannot hold you fast."

It was during the Feast of Dedication that this encounter is set. That is telling, when one remembers the Abomination of Desolation inflicted upon the people during the wretched reign of Antioches Epiphanes in the second-century BC. The nature of the work that Jesus would do for the people would be an act of deliverance. As the Maccabbees delivered the people from the foreign overlords, God would deliver his people from their fiercest enemies: sin and death. As Judas Maccabeus recaptured the Holy City and cleansed the temple from the defilement of Antioches (sacrificing a pig on the altar), Jesus would reclaim the hearts of God's people and wash them pure from sin through the power of forgiveness so that death could not snatch ("take away forcefully") them away from God's intentions. One could read this reference in a predestinarian way, or one could read it with the heart of a pastoral counselor, assuring the believer that in faith one can have the confidence that whatever happens, one is ultimately in the care of God. There is a realism here that can admit, "We know not what the future holds," while at the same time adhere to the certainty, "but we know who holds the future."

When Jesus said, "I and the Father are one" (10:30), a line was drawn in the sand. On the one side, there would be those who heard blasphemy. No human can claim oneness with the almighty! Such an assertion must be silenced, by death if necessary. On the other side, there would be those with ears to hear who would discern the very voice of God trumpeting a remarkable development in the self-revelation of the almighty. Jesus talks about how the love of God is like that of a good shepherd who is willing to lay down his life for the sheep (John 10:11-15). In that act of self-giving, self-sacrificing love, a quality of life is transferred to the believer. This quality of life can only be described as life eternal. It is a quality of life that has dimensions beyond the three we experience spatially in the flesh. Jesus begins to define what this "beyond" means by describing its non-perishing attribute. It is not that one will not die in the sense of all living organisms who come to the end of their life's energy either through accident or natural decline. It is that one will not be lost to God. The image of not being snatched from God's hand contains within it the sense of safety and protection, of endurance and valuation due to the simple fact that God holds that life in a fourth and fifth (?) dimension beyond our current comprehension. The raising of Lazarus, described in the next chapter (John 11), is but a foreshadowing of what the resurrection of the dead will be, for Lazarus will surely die again and like the rest of us will have to wait until the final day when the dead will be raised imperishable. We will need to look to Jesus' resurrection to begin to get a glimpse of what that may mean for us. Here we need to return to the Easter and post-Easter narratives along with Paul's insights in 1 Corinthians 15.

One of the verities of the Christian faith is that as we follow the Good Shepherd in life and in death, we shall be safe. This is the essential message of the two visual images in this text: the first being one of the sheep who follow Jesus and the second being in the Father's hand from which no one will snatch the believer.

Application

Prayer can work miracles. When Peter prayed, he accessed the very power of the risen Lord Jesus and was able to apply that power for the benefit of Tabitha. This is a strong witness to the effectiveness of prayer. We do not know of how many other situations there may have been for Peter and the disciples when they prayed and gained no specific response as dramatic as the raising of Tabitha or the healing of Aeneas. We would certainly be able to identify with them in *this* regard, for all the apparently unanswered prayers we offer over our sick and dying and dead.

How do we understand this? Do we have to extrapolate a theory of dispensation? Or do we chastise the potential recipient or benefactor for lack of faith to receive or convey the miracle? Or do we look for other ways in which God is actively bringing life to the "dying and dead," allegorizing our experience into wisdom or truth propositions? In light of the resurrection of our Lord and Savior, we remain uneasy with the status quo of life as it seems to be lived. After all, God is able to work wonders. Whether God will do so in some demonstrative way in our lives or in the lives of those for whom we care remains to be seen. In faith, we pray and wait and hope. Perhaps that in itself is the miracle and the sign to the world that God is indeed to be taken seriously. This praying, waiting, and hoping is also the posture that prepares us to receive our living Lord rightly when he does show his mercies and when he will come again.

Until he comes again, our world will continue to be a bloody place. A movie in which a group of young people are placed on an island was released in Japan. Only one will be able to come off the island — the one left alive, the survivor. The game plan in everyone's mind is simply to kill before being killed. It is *Lord of the Flies* revisited with a vengeance! Will Freddie Kruger become an "also ran" in the Hall of Flame into which such incendiary movies, depicting the baseness and depravity of human spirit, will be relegated? Blood, whether splashed across the big screen or onto the streets, makes quite a mess. It is a sign of the tragedy of human existence where there is so much suffering and death.

What the world needs is less hurt and more hope! That is precisely what God gives the world in Jesus. He takes our human hurts upon himself — the wounded, bloodied lamb — and offers us a vision of God and ourselves that transcends the reality we have come to think as normal. It transcends it by allowing us to see the majesty of God (a la the seer of Revelation) expressed best through the lamb. Because of what the lamb has done for us, it is true that all "blessing and glory and wisdom and thanksgiving and honor and power and might" (7:12) properly belong to God. We can lay no claim on these attributes, try as we may to create a *new world order*. It is only when we finally learn to live beyond our self, beyond our community, beyond our world, serving God (7:15) and his purposes in the world, that we will penultimately find shelter in the maddening pace from day to day until that final day, when we will ultimately find our eternal rest by those "springs of living water" (7:17).

Reflect on the question that was asked of Jesus: "How long will you keep us in suspense?" (10:24). We love suspense. It will lure us to pay big bucks to go to the theater. It will keep us watching the serial soaps in the afternoon or evening hour after hour, week after week, to see what will develop. Yet we do not like too much suspense, especially when it comes to important matters, like who will be president of the United States. Suspense is really only enjoyable when we have resolve. Until then, it can feel like we are bursting (sometimes painfully), wanting to know how it will all turn out. Jesus' questioners wanted a resolution to the suspense. However, the word (God's answer) works slowly and mysteriously. The "plainly" that they wanted for the communication was complex and cumbersome; the word was wrapped up in humanity and in one-on-one caring and in words tumbling down a mountainside in parables and hard sayings reinterpreting the Law of Moses and in gasps of a dying Master alone on a cross.

Part of the mystery in the working of the word is that any questioner needs to hear in order to believe but also needs to belong in order to hear. How important it is to belong to a Christian congregation in order to be in a position to be exposed regularly to the word through worship, Bible study, fellowship, and service! *And* how important for every congregation to be alert to the questions and problems of daily life that drive people to seek the deep and abiding answers that God's word provides. Yet, in the end, faith itself, knowing oneself to be a sheep of the Good Shepherd, is a gift. It is not a "logical conclusion" at the end of a set of questions and answers. It is more like the experience of being *held*, which an infant knows to the marrow when cradled by the loving parent. This is a foretaste of that quality of eternal life in which believers will know themselves to be secure in the embrace of God for temporal life and through momentary death and into an imperishable eternity.

All things new and improved

We don't much care for new things being forced on us, but we do like to have new things offered to us.

When something new is forced upon us, we have a kind of gag reflex that rejects the new and unfamiliar thing as an unwelcome change. We like to be able to chew on something before we have to swallow it. (We recognize and indulge this in ourselves, even though we often resent it in our congregations.)

When something new is offered to us, on the other hand, we are naturally drawn to it. Even if we had not previously felt dissatisfied with our "old" version, the offer of something new makes the old seem somehow inferior. Of course, in our age of continual upgrades of computer software and hardware, we are encouraged to believe that our old version is, indeed, inferior.

As consumers, we are particularly fond of "new." The word "new" has been married for so long to the word "improved" in our culture that we have come to assume that they always go together. And often they do.

Even beyond our consumerism, we're grateful for the freshness and hope that come with a new season, a new semester, a new year. We find that a new coat of paint surprisingly rejuvenates a room or a house. Some of us feel inwardly renewed by having a new haircut or by wearing new clothes. We like the fresh start of a new job or of life in a new community. And we often wish that we could create that appealing new and clean feeling in some of our old, continuing responsibilities and relationships.

God offers something new. Indeed, in the end, God offers everything new. New and decidedly improved. And that's good news for us — good news for us to hear, and good news for us to proclaim.

Acts 11:1-18

Marketing experts have made a science of determining how many different times — and, for that matter, in how many different ways — a consumer needs to hear a message in order for it to make an impact. But before Madison Avenue was trying to get through to us, God was trying to get through to us. And it seems that God, too, must communicate his message at multiple times and in various ways before we get it.

In the rooftop episode preceding this passage, Peter was a hard sell for the message that God was trying to convey to him. Then, in this passage, the same truth that broke through to Peter finally dawned on Peter's critics. That truth was that God wanted to include the Gentiles because salvation through faith in Christ was available for them too.

Ironically, before the Gentiles could be converted to Christ, Christ's own followers needed something of a conversion. They had to change their thinking, their paradigm, before the gospel could go out into the Gentile world. It's an unnerving thought that — then or now — God's work is delayed because of God's own people. Surely he expects opposition to his work from a sinful world. What a tragedy, though, when opposition comes from his own workers.

God desired to do his work among the Gentiles, but the early church was initially reticent. They were stuck in an old understanding — perhaps even an old misunderstanding — that prohibited the Jews from much contact with the Gentiles. Even the very term used in this passage — Gentiles — reflects the fundamental us/them mentality of the early Jewish Christians.

It's not as though this rooftop revelation to Peter was a new directive from God and the early church just didn't get the memo. Quite the contrary, God had indicated again and again his desire to include the nations (which is literally the meaning of the Hebrew term, *gowy*, from which comes the Yiddish terms *goy* or *goyim* for Gentiles).

Back in Genesis, God chose the family of Abraham to be his own special people. But that choice was embracing, not excluding. God's expressed desire was not merely to bless that family, but through that chosen family "all the families of the earth" (Genesis 12:3) and "all the nations of the earth" (Genesis 18:18) would be blessed.

The Psalms prophesy that "all the nations" will one day worship God (Psalm 22:2; 86:9), and the Psalmist calls on the faithful to proclaim the goodness of God among the nations and all peoples (96:3), and all the nations themselves are called on to praise the Lord (117:1).

God's global good will is made still clearer in the words and works of the Old Testament prophets. God's expressed plan for Jerusalem was not merely to be the holy city for his people only, but for all people, all nations (e.g., Jeremiah 3:17; Micah 4:1-2), and the temple, too, was to be "a house of prayer for all peoples" (Isaiah 56:7). Jerusalem, God's people, and God's servant are all variously given the assignment of being a light and guide to the nations (e.g., Isaiah 49:6; 60:3), and that with the purpose "that my salvation may reach to the end of the earth" (Isaiah 49:6).

Isn't it interesting that Peter himself took some convincing on this point? Back on the Day of Pentecost, Peter had quoted the prophet Joel to explain the work of God, including the promise that God would pour out his Spirit "on all flesh." Still, what Peter understood in theory on the Day of Pentecost was hard to accept as reality in the house of Cornelius.

For the crowds in Jerusalem on the Day of Pentecost, the manifestation of the Spirit was not self-evident proof enough, and so Peter had to validate what was going on by citing scripture (the Joel prophecy). Meanwhile, for the early church in this episode, their own scriptures were not enough to make them understand that God's good plan included the Gentiles. They needed to see (or to hear that Peter had seen) the manifestation of the Spirit there in Cornelius' house.

Revelation 21:1-6

The way the Bible starts makes sense to us: "In the beginning." That's a good, logical place to start. We have our notions of where or how any particular thing is supposed to start. The introduction and preface lay the groundwork at the beginning of the book, not at the end. The overture precedes and anticipates the rest of the performance. The syllabus is handed out on the first day of class, not the last.

Here, in the penultimate chapter of the Bible, however, we are surprised to discover what sounds like an introduction, an overture. Right where we expect to find an ending, we find instead a new beginning.

What a strange time to start something new: at the end. What author writes an introduction at the end of the book? What coach implements a new game plan as the game clock ticks down to zero? Yet here we are introduced to an entire array of newness. There's a new heaven — was there something wrong with the old one? — and a new earth, as well, complete with a new Jerusalem.

The newness God promises is not merely new surroundings. A dysfunctional family, after all, can move into a new house, but the new surroundings do not make their patterns of relating new. So God's promised newness is not merely new environs but new everything.

The new arrangement includes the beautiful image that God's dwelling will no longer be far off, but "with them." Surely scripture affirms God's presence with his people throughout but still there was always a recognition that his throne and his dwelling were off in heaven. No more. This is new.

Likewise, we find here that lovely image of comfort, which so many of us have quoted in hospital rooms and funeral homes along the way. "He will wipe every tear from their eyes." Some gospel songs have rejoiced in the prospect that there will be no more tears, no more crying in that day ("mourning and crying and pain will be no more"). But the promise here is one step sweeter than that. The testimony is not merely that tears will be gone, but specifically God will wipe them away. It is a personal and tender act of comforting by God, and it is an embodiment of his making things new. God is not a sleight of hand magician who waves a magic wand and says "Abracadabra" to make tears go away. Rather he is a loving parent who makes the tears go away by wiping them away himself.

The final specific piece of newness mentioned in this passage is the absence of death. "Death will be no more." Death, in scripture, is a more comprehensive thing than the mere cessation of brain and organ functions. From the day that Adam and Eve ate the fatal fruit but kept on walking and living, we discovered that death is something deeper and more pervasive than just the end point on a person's time line. We as Christians should be particularly aware of this truth, since we also understand that life is something more than just the continuance of brain and organ functions (see, for example, John 3:16; 6:47-51; 11:25-26).

Taken all together, this passage is a great affirmation of the goodness of God's original creation. What is promised and portrayed here is not new in the sense of being different. If I go to a restaurant where I always order the same thing and one day say, "I think I'll try something new," then I mean that I will order something different. What God promises here, however, is not new-different, but new-renewed. It's not something different from or other than heaven and earth and Jerusalem, but rather a new heaven, new earth, new Jerusalem. God's desire to dwell among his people is certainly nothing new for Emmanuel. And the promise of a painless, tearless, and deathless reality is a return to the way God originally created and intended it to be.

John 13:31-35

Present your people with this statement by Jesus, but don't tell them where it comes in the gospel or in the story: "Now the Son of Man has been glorified, and God has been glorified in him." Ask your people when they suppose Jesus said those words and not many are likely to place it at this point in the story.

Perhaps as Jesus enters Jerusalem on Palm Sunday, amid that ancient ticker tape parade, we might imagine Jesus saying, "Now the Son of Man has been glorified." Or when the crowd is eager to crown him king following the feeding of the 5,000, or at his transfiguration, or at the empty tomb.

There are a number of good, natural choices, but John 13 is not one of them. Just a few minutes earlier, Jesus was crouched down at his disciples' feet, his hands in the dirty wash water, performing a servant's function. And, just moments before he makes his "glorified" statement, he has watched one of his chosen twelve disappear into the night to betray him.

Now the Son of Man has been glorified? I'm sorry, but what did I miss?

It seems apparent that Jesus defines "glorified" differently than we do. Jesus does not use this word in any of the synoptic gospels, but it is something of a theme in the gospel of John. Jesus talks about glorification on three occasions (8:54; 11:4; 12:23, 28) prior to John's extended Last Supper scene. And in the dialogues, monologues, and prayer that make up that Last Supper section of John, Jesus makes repeated reference to glorification (13:31-32; 14:13; 15:8; 16:14; 17:1, 4-5, 10).

The theme and theology of glory in the gospel of John deserve more attention than can be given here. For preaching purposes, however, it is worth noting that "glorify" is evidently not something a person can do for himself. As I cannot tickle myself, someone else has to do it, so too I cannot glorify myself. Jesus says as much in 8:54, and he demonstrates it in his later references. His aim is not to glorify himself but to glorify the Father (e.g., 13:31; 14:13; 15:8; 17:4), he is glorified by the Father (13:32; 16:14; 17:1; 17:5), and both the Father and Son are potentially glorified by Jesus' followers (15:8; 17:10).

Jesus addresses those with him as "little children." Our common association with that phrase and

Jesus, of course, is his "let the little children come to me" statement in the synoptics (Matthew 19:14; Mark 10:14; Luke 18:16). The Greek word (*paidion*) used there, however, is not the same as what appears (*teknion*) in this passage. Both are translated "little children" in the NRSV, although *teknion* never actually is used in reference to children in its several New Testament appearances. In addition to this one instance in the gospel of John — the only time Jesus uses the term — Paul uses it as a term of parental endearment and concern with the Galatians (4:19), and it is found seven different times in the five chapter epistles of 1 John.

So in the larger scope of the Last Supper scene in John, Jesus identifies his relationship to his disciples as teacher, lord, master, and model of servitude (13:12-17), as the vine to their branches (15:1-10), and as a friend (15:12-15). Here, in his use of *teknion*, Jesus suggests a kind of tender parental concern for his followers.

The tender term precedes the hard (and, to the disciples, bewildering) news that "I am with you only a little longer" and "where I am going, you cannot come." Both of those unhappy statements, however, are ameliorated later, as Jesus promises to send the Spirit in his absence (16:7), as well as to return for them so that they can be where he is (14:1-3).

Finally, Jesus concludes this section with a "new commandment," though at first blush the commandment to love does not seem new at all (see, for example, Luke 10:27 and Leviticus 19:18). What's new about this commandment, however, is its standard for love (see Alternate Application below).

Application

Call it "Covenant (Version 2.0)." The original covenants with the Old Testament people of God involved almost exclusively one group of people — the descendants of Abraham, Isaac, and Jacob. They were marked by the circumcision-sign of the covenant, and they carried in their Ark the terms of their covenant. Now, however, the God who had for centuries promised that a new covenant was coming (see, for example, Jeremiah 31:31) had put the product on the shelf. Characterized by the mercy of its maker, this covenant was extended to all people. They would be marked by his Spirit, and the terms of the covenant would be written on their hearts. That's surely new and improved.

Call it "Command (Version 2.0)." Centuries before the query prompted the parable of the good Samaritan (see Luke 10:25-37) or the disciples sat around the Passover meal with Jesus, God instructed his people on how to love one another: "as yourself" (Leviticus 19:18). But now, after extended and concentrated time of knowing and being with Jesus, and on the eve of his "greater love has no man" act, Jesus issues a new version of the love command: not to love "as you love yourself," but rather "as I have loved you." That's surely new and improved.

Finally, call it "Creation (Version 2.0)." The God who made heaven and earth makes a new heaven and a new earth. The God who made everything good in the beginning makes everything good again. And the God who made everything makes everything new: new and improved.

An Alternative Application

John 13:31-35. A common unit of measure in Bible times was the cubit. Those of us who grew up reading the King James or Revised Standard Versions will remember the familiar description of Noah's ark being so many cubits high, so many wide, and so many long. Likewise, later, with the story of Solomon's temple.

When we translate into contemporary measurements, we generally approximate a cubit as eighteen inches, for it was reckoned as the distance from a man's elbow to the tip of his middle finger. Of course, that makes the cubit a varying measure. I have a gentleman in my congregation who is 7' 2" tall. His cubit is longer than most.

If I asked all the folks in my church to break out their rulers, tape measures, and yardsticks to measure the altar rail at the front of our church, I daresay that they would all come up with the same figure. If, however, I asked all the folks in my church to measure our altar rail in cubits, then we would end up with very different figures. How many cubits long a thing is depends upon whose cubit you're using.

At the Last Supper scene in the gospel of John, Jesus told his disciples that the time had come to use a new cubit.

The issue at hand is the measurement of love. The standard human measurement had been a flawed and fluctuating one — I will love you the way that you love me. Then Jesus, reiterating the standard of the Old Testament law, commended a higher measure — I will love you the way I love myself. The demand was significantly higher, though the measure was still flawed and imprecise.

On the night before he was crucified, Jesus raised the bar once more. "Just as I have loved you, you also should love one another." Now I will not merely love you the way that you love me, for I will love you even if you hate me. Now I will not merely love you the way that I love myself, for I will love you at the expense of myself. Now I will love you the way that Jesus loved me. Now we are using his cubit.

Easter 6
Acts 16:9-15
Revelation 21:10, 22—22:5
John 14:23-29
David Kalas

Guess who's at the door

It's a picture of God that we see again and again throughout the pages of scripture.

We see it in the familiar story of the shepherd who leaves the 99 in order to pursue the one lost lamb. Again, a few verses later, we see it in the father running to meet his prodigal son. We see it also in the cherished portrait of Jesus standing at the door and knocking. And we see it most dramatically in the Bethlehem stable. It is a picture of a God who comes to us.

It is not a rare thing. Indeed, it so prevalent a pattern in scripture that we might not even notice it!

In the beginning, the Lord comes walking in the Garden of Eden. And, in the wake of Cain's failure, the Lord comes to counsel him. He comes to visit Abraham with good news. He comes to the rescue of the Hebrews in slavery. He comes in an awesome display at Sinai in Moses' day and at the temple in Solomon's day. He comes to meet Paul on the road to Damascus. And he promises to come to us again.

Even though our gospel lection predicts Jesus' departure, still there remains a dramatic promise of his coming. Indeed, perhaps the most surprising and dramatic coming of all.

Acts 16:9-15

We are reminded all along of the variety of means by which God communicates with people. Here, we read that "Paul had a vision," and he and his companions understood it as direction from God. Elsewhere, God's word is brought by angels, by prophets, by preachers, and even by a donkey. He gives dreams and the interpretation of dreams. He inspires otherworldly utterances, as well as the interpretation of those utterances. He writes on walls, thunders from mountains, and remains the still, small voice.

In this particular instance, it seems that God is giving direction to his missionaries. On this, Paul's second missionary journey, the team has focused their attention in Asia Minor, which was Paul's boyhood home, as well as the region where he spent most of his first missionary journey. Then comes this vision of a man from Macedonia, across the Aegean Sea from Asia Minor.

That Paul's vision came during the night serves as an interesting metaphor. During his waking hours when his eyes were open, it seems, the apostle was not seeing much beyond the confines of the immediate mission field there in Asia Minor. So the Lord took the occasion of Paul's sleep to expand the horizons of his vision and work. There were other souls to be reached — souls on the other side of the Aegean — and that vision in the night prompted a whole new move in Paul's missionary work.

The crossing of the Aegean was, in Neil Armstrong's famous phrase, "one small step for man." It was a more significant step for the church, however, as Paul's missionary effort entered Europe, the Greek peninsula, and moved a step closer to Rome itself.

The book of Acts itself also takes a significant step at this point. Suddenly, the narrator steps on stage and becomes one of the characters in the story. Everything up until this point has been written in the third person, but in 16:10 the language abruptly shifts to first-person, plural. "We" becomes the operative word for the next several verses as Luke himself becomes part of the team. Neither Luke here, nor Paul elsewhere, elaborates on how the two met or on Luke's participation in Paul's itinerary. Based on the pronouns used, it seems to have been very brief at this stage, though we know from later references that Luke became a more constant companion of Paul near the end.

On the other side of the Aegean, we see no evidence of missionary activity in Neapolis. Instead, the action moves almost immediately to Philippi. Luke reports that the group went "where we supposed there was a place of prayer" on the sabbath day. This move reflects Paul's pattern of going first to the Jews in any given place to preach the gospel to them. That they were forced to look for "a place of prayer," however, suggests that there weren't enough Jews in Philippi to establish or maintain a synagogue. The place of prayer was the alternative, informal meeting place in the absence of an official synagogue.

Interestingly, it appears that only women were gathered in that makeshift congregation on that sabbath day.

Among the four gospel writers, Luke is known as the one who is most attentive to the role of women in the story. Likewise, here in the book of Acts, the women are the ones who are holding the fort in Philippi. Lydia is often thought of as the first Christian convert on European soil. It is Lydia's hospitality that supports Paul and his companions during the time in Philippi, which is reminiscent of the women who provided for Jesus during his ministry (see, for example, Matthew 27:55). It was a woman whose liberation from her demon-possession is the hinge on which the rest of the story in Philippi turns.

Luke identifies Lydia here as "a worshiper of God," just as he does Titius Justus later (Acts 18:7). An almost identical reference is also made to Cornelius earlier (Acts 10:2, 22). The strong implication is that Lydia was a Gentile who had come to worship the God of the Jews. She has already demonstrated, therefore, an open and receptive spirit: open to hear something that she hadn't heard before, and to receive that new truth into her life. So she, like Cornelius before, completes her journey: first to the worship of the Father and then to the salvation in his Son.

Luke reports that Lydia "and her household were baptized." Later in Paul's eventful stay in Philippi, Luke tells us that the jailer "and his entire family were baptized." It is, in both instances, a beautiful image. Rather than the convert living his or her newfound faith in isolation and living in a divided household, we see the entire household coming to Christ. Like the Samaritan woman whose contact with Christ led her entire village to believe in him (John 4:39-42), Lydia and the jailer did not merely respond to the gospel themselves; they brought their households with them.

Finally, the episode concludes with a kind of metaphor for the relationship between faith and works. Lydia opens her home to Paul and his companions and in the end it seems that her home becomes the gathering place for all of the new believers there in Philippi (see Acts 16:40). Her household is not only baptized, representing their faith, but her home is also opened to others in hospitality, representing good works.

Revelation 21:10, 22—22:5

The city that wants to attract tourists will put together promotional materials boasting all that the city has. The recreation, the culture, and the entertainment; shopping and dining; convenience and cleanliness: these are the types of things that a city might claim to have and to offer.

Near the end of the book of Revelation, John offers a very different sort of promotion of the city he has in mind. His subject is "the holy city Jerusalem."

We are introduced to Jerusalem early and often in scripture, but King David is the man who really puts it on the map. He conquers it, makes it his capital, and then effectively makes it God's capital by moving the Ark of the Covenant there. A generation later, Solomon cements it as God's dwelling place, building the glorious temple there.

As the years pass, Jerusalem becomes a city like no other. Not that it is the biggest or the highest or the wealthiest (except, perhaps, in the gilded days of Solomon). Rather, it gains an ethos as the center of God's activity. The accumulated testimony of the prophets is that his glory, his throne, and his eternal purpose are there. All peoples and nations will come to worship the Lord who dwells in Zion. And while the northern kingdom was allowed to slip away between history's cracks, David's throne in Jerusalem will always have one of his descendants on it. One day, some particular son of David will reign there in uncommon strength, justice, peace, and security forever.

I saw a map once from the sixteenth century that depicted the world as a kind of three-petal flower. The one petal, stretching from the center to the northwest, was labeled "Europe." A second petal, growing down from the center to the south, was labeled "Africa." The third petal, reaching out from the center to the northeast, was labeled "Asia." And in the middle of the flower, the center of the world: Jerusalem.

A modern cartographer would not endorse such a map of the world, but a theologian might. Scripture surely paints a picture in which Jerusalem emerges as the center of the world. Here in our passage, a new Jerusalem is depicted as the perfect culmination of God's will for the world.

John's promotion of the city is an unconventional one. Rather than boasting about what the city has, he makes a point of identifying what it does not have.

The city has no temple (21:22). At first blush, that might seem a negative thing. In contrast to the quaint little towns where there was a church on every corner, this city might seem like a godless place with no temple at all. But, no; quite the opposite.

John also suggests that the city has no sun or moon (21:23) or lamps (22:5). Who would want to go to such a dark and dreary place? Our culture is drawn to the bright lights and neon of Broadway, South Beach, or Vegas. But what sort of low-watt city is this? It is, it seems, the most radiant spot in the universe, "for the glory of God is its light."

The city has no nightlife on the one hand (22:5), but neither does it ever shut down (21:25). And, for would-be residents, see the quality of life implied by what is missing there: "nothing unclean," no one "who practices abomination or falsehood," and "nothing accursed."

Ask a broken and discouraged person what they would change about their circumstances, and chances are that they will speak in terms of what things they'd like to be rid of. No more pain in their bodies. No more fighting in their marriages. No more violence in their homes. No more lies, no more alcohol, no more strife. On and on the list goes, and you could add to it from the parishioners you've counseled.

For the weary inhabitants of a fallen world, John's list of what will not be part of the new Jerusalem is very good news, indeed. The news gets better still, for the vision is not just a glimpse of what's missing but also an assurance of what's there. The passage is laced with one great, recurring promise: the glorious presence of God and of the lamb.

John 14:23-29

Our selected gospel lection comes from the midst of John's Last Supper scene. The synoptics' accounts of this event are comparatively short, while John shares with us a great deal more dialogue and monologue (and even a bit more action in the form of the foot washing) than his counterparts. Several of the prominent themes from John's Last Supper section are represented here in this excerpt from it.

Love is a central theme of the Johannine literature in general. John's gospel, after all, is the one that offers the great "for God so loved" summary of the good news. It also includes the new love commandment (John 13:34) and the author's self-identification as "the disciple whom (Jesus) loved" (see, for example, John 19:26). Jesus tells his disciples that love is the ultimate evidence that they belong to him (John 13:35). Meanwhile, one cannot read John's first epistle without being struck by the central role of love. It is the essence of God's nature (4:8b), the proof of our relationship to him (3:10; 4:20-21), and the practical living out of that relationship (3:16-18).

It is within that larger thematic context, then, that we meet this particular passage. Here the causal relationship presented is between love and obedience. "Those who love me will keep my word," Jesus says.

That relationship is not a two-way street. Obeying God does not automatically lead to loving God, as many a grim legalist has demonstrated. Loving the Lord ought to manifest itself naturally in keeping his word. If it does not, the professed love is likely to be shallow or altogether counterfeit.

A second significant theme, in this selection and in its larger context, is the glimpse we are given of the Trinity. This is a real gift of the fourth gospel.

Of course, Jesus does not present us with a systematic theology on the three persons of the Trinity. But then, he shouldn't. The Father and the Spirit are not objects of study for Jesus; they are his loved ones. Rather than a philosophical discourse, we are given a peek into a loving relationship.

While Jesus speaks a very great deal about the Father throughout the gospels, this Last Supper scene from John's gospel is our best opportunity to hear him speak about the Father and the Spirit. We discover several themes that are also explicit in this particular excerpt.

One: the theme of sending. The Father sent the Son, and the Father and/or the Son will send the Spirit. (Similarly, it should be noted that the Son also sends the disciples.)

Two: there is a pattern of the members of the Trinity focusing attention on one another, glorifying one another, and even arguably serving one another; while the focus is never on themselves. While this pattern is more explicitly fleshed out in the larger context, it is surely indicated here by the Spirit's purpose being to remind the disciples of everything Jesus had said (v. 26) and by Jesus' deference to the Father (v. 28).

Three: there is the theme of a certain relationship between the disciples and the Trinity. Jesus' followers are not merely on the outside looking in but rather there is a more intimate connection (or opportunity). Elsewhere, Jesus' prayer is that the unity of the disciples would be like the unity of the Trinity. Also, as we mentioned above, the disciples become a kind of extension of the Trinity as they are the next ones being sent. Here in our passage, there is the marvelous promise from the Trinity to Christ's followers: "We will come to them and make our home with them."

Four: finally, a theme that is significant in John's Last Supper scene — and well represented in this excerpt from it — is the prospect of Jesus going away.

It's hard to know for sure the state of mind of Jesus' disciples on this occasion. On the one hand, he had spoken plainly to them on several occasions about what would happen to him in Jerusalem. On the other hand, how could they possibly be expected to understand such things in advance of them happening? I can tell my five-year-old daughter about some elements of life that will confront her when she goes off to college, but I should not expect her to grasp my words and their meaning at this stage of the game.

Now his departure is very much at hand, whether the disciples grasp it or not. Yet, in both this passage and this larger section of John, Jesus portrays his going away as a positive thing. It is best for him, and it is best for them.

Application

That God should come to us at all is itself remarkable. He should have turned his back on us and walked away back in the Garden of Eden. And again and again since then. Instead, he comes to us. Like a concerned shepherd, like a forgiving father, as a baby referred to as Emmanuel, he comes to us.

Now, in the lections from John and Revelation, we are presented with two more remarkable images of his coming.

First, there is the personal, individual coming. The NRSV translates the whole promise as plural — "those who love me" — in order to be inclusive. In the original Greek, however, it is expressed in the singular. So the New King James Version reads, "If anyone loves me, he will keep my word; and my Father will love him, and we will come to him and make our home with him" (John 14:23 NKJV).

It is an astonishingly intimate image. That the Father should send his Son into the world because he so loves the world is surprising, but at least it is the "big picture." Here, however, it is unimaginably personal: the triune God will come to and dwell with me. You. Anyone who loves him and keeps his word.

In the Revelation passage, we see the other astonishing truth of his coming. While Caesar is famous for saying, "I came, I saw, I conquered," the Lord has said a more dramatic thing. He promises to come, and then he promises to stay. Central to the picture of the new Jerusalem is the abiding presence and glory of God. He dwells there with his people. So this God does not just come to see, to visit, or to conquer. He comes to stay.

An Alternative Application

Acts 16:9-15. "Faith of Our Mothers, Living Still." While we don't know anything specifically about Lydia as a mother — including whether she even was a mother — her example may be a good one.

First, we have good reason to infer that she was an exceedingly capable woman, apparently running her own business. One senses that she may have embodied the strong and able woman described in Proverbs 31.

Second, we see that she was a devout woman. In the absence of any synagogue to support her in her adopted faith, still she was there at the place of prayer with other devout women.

Finally, as we noted above, Lydia's conversion was not a solitary event. Conversion never should be, of course. It is not much of a rock if it doesn't make any ripple. But Lydia's conversion was accompanied by good works. In an act that makes her an especially appropriate hero for this day, we see that Lydia set a pace of conversion and belief for her entire household.

Ascension of Our Lord
Acts 1:1-11
Ephesians 1:15-23
Luke 24:44-53
Mark Molldrem

Jesus rules!

In golf, Tiger rules. In tennis, Venus. Depending upon which teen you talk with, any teen idol rules. In America, the people rule, despite what some political cynics or party technocrats say. For Christians wherever, Jesus rules!

One might think that such a theme would more appropriately be served on Christ the King Sunday. That is at the end of the Pentecost season, six months away. The festival day of the Ascension is just as appropriate to lift up the reality of the lordship of Jesus. Viewed from the perspective of the church calendar, this day effectively closes out the "season of Christ," celebrating his position in the divine economy as it culminates his work on earth. (Christ the King Sunday closes out the "season of the church" by accenting the role of Christ in relationship to the church and the cosmos.)

An underlying question that begs our sincere attention is this: What has gained ascendency in our lives today, threatening to replace Jesus in our hearts?

Acts 1:1-11

Everybody loves a sequel, especially if the first part was so good! Sometimes the follow-up story, however, leaves one wanting; but not in this case. Luke knows a good market when he sees it. Two thousand years of history have proven him right. "In the first book, O Theophilus...." Luke penned his gospel of the acts of Jesus, not just because everybody was doing it, but to give "an orderly account" (Luke 1:3); and, not just for the sake of the truth, but "that you may know the truth" (Luke 1:4) about Jesus — the you referring to any Theophilus, lover of God, who may be reading the book. The knowing does not mean intellectual abstraction about God but personal attachment to God.

Now, with the return of Jesus apparently delayed (see 1:11) and so many great things happening before his very eyes, Luke does not want the acts of the apostles to be misunderstood or forgotten. So, he takes pen in hand once again and constructs a narrative that could just as easily be titled "The Acts of the Holy Spirit." It is designed to make sense to anyone who is already familiar with the story of Jesus; yet, it is told in such a way that even those unfamiliar with Jesus are introduced to him through the sermons and personal testimonies laced throughout the account. Many are brought to faith through the faithful witness of the disciples, who are empowered by the Holy Spirit. The church grows, demonstrating in its daily life what believers do while they are waiting for their Lord to return.

Structurally, these introductory verses in Acts are linked to the closing verses in Luke. Luke's account of the commissioning of the disciples as witnesses (Luke 24:44-49) is recapped in Acts 1:1-5. Then, the ascension, related briefly in Luke 24:50-53, is expanded upon in Acts 1:6-11. How the disciples got out of the temple, where they were "continually... blessing God" (Luke 24:53), is what the book of Acts is all about, beginning with the Pentecost experience and spreading out into the streets of Jerusalem, onto the roads into Asia Minor, and across the waters to Rome.

Consistent with his propensity to locate his narrative in verifiable history with public figures, Luke uses the term proof 1:3 to refer to the post-resurrection appearances of Jesus. This word carries a different sense than (witness), in that a witness or testimony would emphasize the person's perspective on the subject, whereas "proof" conveys the sense of credible evidence on its own merits. A witness would say, "Jesus is the risen Savior of the world." A proof would say, "Jesus walked on the path toward Emmaus at 6:00 p.m. Sunday after Passover." Both may refer to the same event but express it differently, one focusing on the meaning and the other on the matter of the experience. In Acts, Luke does not specify the details of these proofs, although in his gospel narrative he recounts the details of the travelers on the road to Emmaus (Luke 24:13-43). Paul delineates several appearances of Jesus after the resurrection in 1 Corinthians 15:3-11; John, in John 20:11-29 and 21:1-23.

Luke passes over the specifics with a reference to the forty days between the resurrection and the ascension, which is his primary focus in transition in these introductory verses. Just as the forty years of wandering in the wilderness was a complete time to judge the people for their faithlessness (Numbers 14:26-35) and just as the forty days of temptation in the wilderness (Matthew 4:1-11; Luke 4:1-13) was a complete time to evidence Jesus' faithfulness, so too is the forty days of post-resurrection life together a complete time to convince the disciples that Jesus is indeed the risen Savior of the world to whom they will witness with the rest of their lives. (Three other significant spans of forty worth remembering, as recorded in scripture, are Genesis 7:1-5, the forty days of rain producing the flood, revealing God's judgment upon the earth; Exodus 24:12-18 and Deuteronomy 9:9-11, the forty days that Moses spent on the mountain receiving the revelation of God through the law; and Jonah 4:3, the forty days given to Nineveh to repent.)

Ephesians 1:15-23

"Paul... by the will of God." These are the words that begin the Letter to the Ephesians. These words thrust us right back into the book of Acts where we read of the conversion of Saul (Acts 9). These words expose the authority and power behind the thoughts, words, and actions of this singular man, who could rightly be called the theologian of the church. Though he did not write a systematics like Aquinas, Barth, or Tillich, he wrote in a few preserved letters more to shape the Christian understanding of the gospel at its heart than all the other writers of Christendom.

Because the Ephesians are (Acts 1:11), in Jesus, Paul is thankfully mindful of them in prayer. His intercession is that they may grow "in the knowledge of him" (1:17), which is richer and more immeasurable than the one extremely long sentence (1:15-23) in which he expressed his thoughts. David H. Stern, in his translation, *Jewish New Testament*, does a nice job of cutting up the meat of Paul's writing into chewable portions. (This or another translation that expresses the meaning of the text in "ear-palatable units" would be preferred by lector and worshiper alike over a reading from anything resembling the Revised Standard Version treatment of the text, as good as it is with the Greek.)

Though Paul is indeed grounded historically in the events of Jesus and the early church, he writes conceptually about them. He asks the question, "What does this mean?" In reference to the ascension that Luke recounts, Paul expresses its meaning. Jesus is not only raised from the dead; he is also intentionally and demonstrably placed at the right hand of God, the place of honor, "in the heavenly places" (1:20; spatially separate from earth, so there is no confusion of conflating heaven and earth into one sphere, making any expression of heaven but a metaphor for an enhanced experience of earth's realm). Jesus has a superior rule "far above all rule and authority and power and dominion" (1:21). As he expresses also in Philippians 2:9-11, Jesus' name exceeds all others; no other name can ascend higher than his. The notion of ruling is again visualized by the world as Jesus' footstool (see Psalm 110:1-2; 1 Corinthians 15:24-27). A final image Paul uses to conceptualize the ascended state of Jesus after the resurrection is that of Jesus as the head of the body. The head fills the body with purpose as it guides its function.

When Paul writes of "the knowledge of him," he is not referring to gnostic knowledge or the secrets of the mystery religions prevalent in his day. He is directing his readers to the saving faith that comes from a personal relationship with Jesus. Notice how many times Paul uses the construct "in him" or "in Christ" in the previous verses to today's text. Because Jesus "fills all in all" (see also Colossians 3:11), believers will find their all in him. The knowledge of Jesus, which comes through a faith relationship with him (trusting his work for our welfare, as expressed in Romans 5:6-11, for example), provides the riches that are the inheritance of the saints of God. These riches are gifts like the forgiveness of sins, the strengthening presence of God, and the hope of eternal life. Paul even says that this faith relationship with Jesus is a gift from God, "the immeasurable greatness of his power in us... according to the working of his great might" (1:19). Faith in Jesus is itself a manifestation of God's power in us.

Luke 24:44-53

Is the ending of Luke's gospel nothing more than what denouement is to the climax of a novel? Or is this actually part of the climax that keeps on building beyond the record and beyond the sequel to the beyond of beyond? The analogy of gospel narrative to story is beneficial only to a point, because the story is decidedly different than either a novel, a docudrama, or even "real TV." We are dealing with God's dealings with the world. That is an ever-unfolding event that certainly has its accents in history (creation, call, exodus, exile, restoration, crucifixion, resurrection), but also holds promise of plot yet to be written. Luke understands this. That is why there is the explanation of consequential expectations to the work of Jesus, namely, repentance and forgiveness of sins, preaching and witnessing, waiting for empowerment from God to be about these very things, and worshiping God with joy in the meantime.

Just like he did with the two travelers on the road to Emmaus, Jesus takes time to help his disciples understand how the scriptures are fulfilled in him. The key is to look in those passages that describe the suffering Messiah (for example, Isaiah 50:6, 52:13—53:12; Psalm 22). What this Messiah will effect is nothing less than the forgiveness of sins, which will set right the relationship with God. This message is not just for a chosen few; it is to be spread to the nations. It may begin in Jerusalem, but it is not to end until it has reached the farthest corners of the world. The power to accomplish this communication feat will not come from within a group of highly successful, self-motivated people. The power will come "from on high" (24:49). There will be — there must be — a divine empowerment to accomplish all this.

Just as the disciples learned to trust Jesus through his ministry with them, they would need to trust him when he gave his word about sending "the promise of my Father" (24:49). The disciples would soon learn that one fulfillment spills over into another. The promises of the Messiah were fulfilled in Jesus, who in turn made promises on behalf of his heavenly Father to send the Holy Spirit (refer to Acts 1:4-5). This promise would soon be fulfilled, as recounted in the opening scenes in the Acts of the Apostles (Acts 2).

Luke concludes his gospel narrative in the same spirit with which he began it: with great joy! The angels announced the mood at the birth of Jesus (Luke 2:10), and the disciples retained the mood after the crucifixion, resurrection, and ascension (24:52). This joy, no doubt, filled each day in delightful ways as they moved in and out of their routines. But one fact stands out in Luke's description of the joyful fellowship of those whose lives had been touched by Jesus. They were "in the temple" worshiping (24:53). The disciples expressed their faith in worshipful acts that had a public and corporate dimension to them. When Jesus addressed them with directions on what to do after he ascended, he spoke to them as a body. The plural form of address is used, both in the imperative verb and the pronoun. Thus, when the Holy Spirit did come upon them, "they were all together in one place" (Acts 1:2).

Application

In our post-modern world, meaning is elusive. The age of absolute faith is past. The age of absolute science is past. The age of absolute history is past. Everything is revised and considered revisable. In our efforts to make sense of an ever-changing sketch, we seek after a line of meaning to connect the dots. If the God who is God does not provide the connections of meaning for one, something else will — whether that be Satanism, occultism, Wicca, amorphous new age spirituality, astrology, voodoo, communism, nationalism, capitalism, or nihilism, to mention a few possibilities.

Jesus presented himself alive to the disciples after his death on the cross, "speaking of the kingdom of God" (1:3). Christians today are to announce to our present world, "Jesus rules!" He is the ascended one, who claims power and authority over the world. He empowers his disciples, then and now, to witness to the meaning of life in his name. Jerusalem was the epicenter at that time, but now the whole world has become the stage on which this pronouncement is to be made. It begins in each particular locality where the church exists and expands in ever-enlarging circles. The empowerment for this to happen comes from God through the Holy Spirit, as the church is emboldened to give witness to the "witness" that is our privilege to believe and steward.

We are living in a time of anarchy of opinion. It is the result of a mindless democratization of values, which leaves citizens in a morass when it comes to making intelligent decisions. Ted Koppel makes this pithy comment in his book *Off Camera: Private Thoughts Made Public*: "The spirit of cultural diversity and political correctness is turning sour. We are in danger, in our efforts to be fair, of acceding to some wrongheaded positions, simply because they are held by someone in a minority group." The practical difficulty of such a situation reveals itself for Christian parents who cannot discern proper family commitments in their weekly schedule. They try to pack it all in and crowd out Jesus, who is to be their "all and in all" (Colossians 3:11). Worship and Christian education (whether Sunday school or confirmation or adult classes) become optional, "skippable," because of other events that "we just need to attend."

The sense of priorities that are determined by the criterion that Jesus is Lord, Jesus rules, must be reclaimed by Christians who are living next to neighbors for whom this is a foreign notion. One of the ways we can publicly witness to our faith is by being certain places at certain times with certain attitudes and behaviors that can speak louder than words. A touchy example of this would be the Christian family who chooses worship and Christian fellowship on a Sunday morning over golf, soccer, hockey, or company. A sticky example of this would be the Christian in a board meeting shaping company policy, not by the bottom line necessarily, but by what is just and equitable for the employees or customers, even if the stockholders have to "bite the bullet" this time. The Third Commandment about the sabbath has as its assumption that Jesus is Lord of the sabbath, and that his lordship extends into every day because of it. In our day, it will probably be more prickly to preach about these things than to preach about being saved by grace. Now, there's a sad commentary on the state of our hearts.

Referring to the state of our hearts, we can ask ourselves if, despite the prosperity of the past years, there is a prosperity of joy in our lives. When we skim across the headlines of our nation and world, observing the continued and growing need for peace, security, quality education, relief from poverty, and the exploitation of children, we must admit that human hearts are easily distracted from the one thing needful — to have and to hold a living relationship with the Lord of life. Sin is the root cause of all that is wrong in our world. The crisis of our human culture is spiritual. Economic policies, educational methods, military posturing, welfare reforms, and legislative initiatives can only go so far in advancing the human agenda. Until there is total surrender to the will of God, there will always be the need for preaching and witnessing.

With the growth of metropolitan areas, which are attracting the population of the world into teeming centers of humanity, the instruction of Jesus takes on a new meaning today: stay in the city. A slogan that has been part of the Evangelical Lutheran Church in America's ministry has been put on promotional buttons and reads: In the City for Good. As Christians work together in the places where humanity is at its thickest, there is strong potential for the Holy Spirit to visit the enterprise "with power from on high." Our troubled cities will benefit from such a concerted effort by the body of Christ, which will discover Christ filling all with himself wherever the heart's eye is focused on him.

Easter 7
Acts 16:16-34
Revelation 22:12-14, 16-17, 20-21
John 17:20-26
Craig MacCreary

Locked in a room with open doors

Years ago, Ernest Campbell, former preaching minister at New York's Riverside Church, titled a volume of sermons *Locked in a Room with Open Doors.* There is hardly a year goes by when I am not drawn to the sermon from which the title of the book was drawn. In the sermon, Campbell covers the many things that hold us back from going through the doors that God has opened for us — the fear of the new, worry, fear of the unknown. The assumption is that we ought to be able to go through the doors that are open to us and that we should deal with what is holding us back. Campbell's point is that while God has opened doors for us there is something that restrains us.

Life often does feel like that. Often when I sit down to my computer I experience this. There always seems to be at least one more program or feature that I need to able to take full benefit of all that I already have. I always seem to be one more download away from bliss or total security. A full life is only an upgrade away. Often some dialogue box will come up with some reason why I cannot fulfill my heart's desire — locked in a room with open doors! I am locked in: at least until I open the door of my computer store and go in to buy the needed update to my computer that will make all upgrades possible. I cringe at the introduction of the latest Microsoft operating system as I ponder what might be withheld from me as a result of failing to buy into all the new possibilities.

The assumption behind Campbell's words, written long before the massive introduction of computers and the internet, is that no one should stay put if they can avoid it. Given the times of social upheaval and challenge in which he was writing, it was clear that one should march through any opening for increased justice and diminished oppression. On this score, Campbell was clearly right. However, in our time there is a case for those who do not go through all the doors that are opened to increased consumption and waste. Staying put and sticking with what you have may be as faithful a response as moving through all the doors that may be open to us.

Each of these texts make a case for remaining where we are without yielding to the temptation of dashing off in all the directions that might be open to us.

What saves the jailor in the Acts text is that Paul and Silas do not exit through the doors that are open to them. Indeed, their witness moves the jailor to open the door to a conversation about salvation. Staying in place has its merits. The heart of the message of the book of Revelation is in a sense, "Stay put, stay on message, and stay at it for Jesus is coming." Of course, the author is living in exile so there was not much alternative to staying put. The situation of the church today might not be all that different from the situation of John of Patmos. How do we stay at it and stay as a presence in the culture when the culture is less likely to affirm or even understand what we are about as a people of faith?

Despite Jesus' plea in the lesson from John that all his people be one, the ecumenical movement has fallen on hard times. It seems, in many ways, we have rushed through a door and crossed a threshold where churches have an increasingly hard time naming or even believing in a fundamental unity. Does Generation X see the same Jesus in the religious life of baby boomers? Can a megachurch member understand the faith life of those congregations with fewer than fifty in attendance on a Sunday morning? Have we crossed a threshold where we find lack of understanding and appreciation for the "varieties of religious

81

presence" in our communities? One might even ask what kind of unity Jesus would pray for amongst Christians, Jews, Muslims, and other faiths. Have we crossed a threshold where we find it hard to hear and speak with one another?

The lectionary this Sunday invites us to consider whether some of the thresholds we have crossed have left us further from or closer to Jesus' intentions.

Acts 16:16-34

Certainly, there is no doubt that in this text Paul opens a door for the demon-possessed slave girl. Of course, in the process, he opens a can of worms, as well. However, it is not uncommon to find that a healing poses some serious challenges. Many families have grown dependent upon having a sick member whose illness the family has grown reliant upon to divert and distract them.

The late Edwin Friedman, family therapist, told stories of his mentor, Murray Bowen, who found that the visit of family members to mentally ill relatives often made their sick relatives worse. He found that from time to time when one member of a family got better another member would manifest the symptoms of the same sickness. It seemed that a family needed at least one sick member to talk about, to blame for their problems, and to divert from doing the hard work of developing healthy patterns amongst themselves. Opening the door almost always opens up challenges in one form or another. It is hardly surprising that the reaction of the slave girl's handlers is less than enthusiastic.

How did Paul come to be such a font of blessing in this situation? We would like to think that this came about as a result of Paul's well-meaning, thoughtful, and faithful understanding. That is not the case. "Paul, very much annoyed, turned and said to the spirit, 'I order you in the name of Jesus Christ to come out of her.' And it came out that very hour." The movement of the Spirit here does not wait for Paul to summon up the appropriate emotional correctness or theological soundness. This seems less than satisfactory.

Sometimes a simple reversal of the equation brings some insight. In this case, annoyance becomes the occasion for opening some doors, which is often a lot better than annoyance being the cause of doors closing. My computer gives anger, frustration, exasperation, and infuriation, as synonyms for annoyance. When things get to that point options for better days begin to close. Certainly, as Paul is portrayed in scripture he is capable of annoyance and all its potential synonyms. Things that are normally negative, beyond the positive of merely venting, are turned into a positive when directed at the demonic. The reader wonders why it took several days for Paul to get to the place where he could lay down the order to the demon to come out of the girl. Was he afraid of being misunderstood showing an interest in the future of a slave girl? Certainly, doors remain closed when our fears of being misunderstood so overwhelm us that we do not say what needs to be said. Perhaps he had to sort through just who he was angry at.

Do we find it easier to be annoyed with people? Are we trying to fix them when we should be using our emotional energy to create an environment in which the demonic can just pour out of them? It is easier to wallow in being annoyed, feeling sorry for ourselves, and blaming God for putting all those frustrating people in our path? It is certainly a lot easier than directing our energies toward casting out the demonic. How often have we stood in the way of what could be done to open doors? It took Paul a while of staying put before he could open any doors.

The net result of what did happen is that Paul and Silas found some doors opening to them, only they were behind jailhouse doors. Knowing that Paul is a Roman citizen, it seems strange that Paul does not play the citizenship card to stay out of jail.

It seems that the plan here is about these doors being open to the ministry of Paul and Silas. Prison is open to them and open to what God is doing. The Lukan author makes it clear that the prisoners were listening to them singing and praying. The faith gains credibility in this scene precisely because the privilege card is not played. Indeed the book of Acts is the story of a church that gains credibility with the least and the most vulnerable. Paul will play his citizenship card but not to get out of jail. He will play the card to get to the magistrates so that they apologize to Paul and back off.

This must have been quite a sight for Paul's fellow prisoners and surely lifted his credibility in their sight. Acts reminds us that Peter the first, the original disciple, stayed with Simon the tanner when he was in Joppa. Of course a tanner was a filthy occupation that was on the low end of the career tract in the ancient world. One wonders if the current churches, mega and mainline, see their plans as measuring faith development in terms of credibility with the least. Have we crossed a threshold that separates many of us from the original plan?

Of course, there is the miraculous earthquake that throws open all the doors and releases the prisoners from their chains. It is a different story for the jailor whose career and life are on the line if all the prisoners escape. Paul and Silas choose to stay put in jail locked in before open doors. One can easily make the case for rushing through the open doors. Certainly this miraculous escape mechanism would be quite an impressive tale to be told in the ancient world.

If Christianity is to be about a magic faith moving from one miracle to the next then dashing through those open doors would be the thing to do. But Paul and Silas are held back by the ethical and moral dimension of the faith. I am reminded of Mahatma Gandhi who refused to hurt the British war effort in World War I because he enjoyed the benefits of living under the British Empire and therefore he had a responsibility for its defense. There are some thresholds that should not be crossed because in the long run they violate what we should be about. Sometimes we should be locked in a room with open doors.

Revelation 22:12-14, 16-17, 20-21

"Blessed are those who wash their robes, so that they will have the right to the tree of life and may enter the city by the gates." This is the promise of the book of Revelation — those who have had their robes washed can enter into the "Holy City, the New Jerusalem" God is bringing about. Revelation 21:25 makes very clear that those who long to enter the gates to this new order of things find that these portals are never closed.

Nevertheless, I don't know a pastor of any theological orientation for whom it feels that way. In every typology of churches there is always the classification that names congregations as mules, cats, or some other creature that is hard to corral and heard. A random sampling of most pastors tends to show that a disproportionate number of them have wound up serving these churches. I know the feeling, yet a caveat is in order here. There is great danger in identifying our pet projects and ideas as the portal through which folks must pass in order to enter the kingdom. We run the risk of being every bit as much a gatekeeper as some of our less progressive and more recalcitrant members. However, the doors are never closed to what kind of wisdom and learning God might bring out of our journey with people who just cannot seem to bring themselves to look at life through our lens.

Revelation makes clear that if there is a block to entering the New Jerusalem, it is internal rather than external. It seems that in our age we have plenty to come clean about if we are to enter the new order of things. The outer garment in which we have wrapped our faith needs a good soak in cleansing water. I bristle at those who see in the cross primarily a vengeful God sacrificing his only son in an orgy of blood sacrifice. My faith is not wrapped up in such an interpretation. Yet, the text says there is a blessing in immersing one's robe in some cleansing. I need to be immersed into the world of those who bring to the cross the experience of being abused.

This passage suggests that a clean, refreshed feeling is a precursor to entering through the gates that are never shut. Often in church we take that to mean primarily a cleansing of our sins. But we can be so dirtied in church that we feel so unclean as to be inhibited from marching right through the open gate. If you are a parent of a child and you are holding down two jobs, insufficiently parented because your parents were holding down two jobs, and you are dealing with a child pumped up on food additives — you don't need to be shamed for your lack of skill in handling your child when they become a nuisance. How do we leave people refreshed enough that they can enter through the gate that leads to the New Jerusalem? Many parents have an accumulation of blood, sweat, and tears trying to fight the good fight with their children.

"The Spirit and the bride say, 'Come.' And let everyone who hears say, 'Come.' And let everyone who is thirsty come. Let anyone who wishes take the water of life as a gift." While that is what the spirit and the bride say, we often have devised ways that say, "come but see footnote at bottom of the page." "Please come as long as you are very much like us and do not tip the balance of our comfort zone." We need to come clean as to how, even despite our best intentions, we have become frenetic gatekeepers of gates that do not need keeping for they are always open.

John 17:20-26

Do you feel yourself freezing up and going into shut down mode when you hear this kind of language? One can certainly feel doors closing when we hear much of the language of the gospel of John. This gospel invites us with such language as John 3:16 and puts us off with language that seems to suggest that Jesus is the only avenue to gain access to heaven because he is "the way the truth and the life." I approach this gospel in anticipation and dread for it seems to have been the source of as many doors closing as hearts opening.

Yet, Jesus' prayer is his petition that all will be able to see his glory. In his narration of Jesus' life, John makes clear that this prayer has been answered in church experience. In the first chapter he tells us that "the word has become flesh and lived among us and we have beheld his glory." Of course, in the gospel the glory can only be apprehended in light of the cross. Yet, it seems that there are certain events that illumine the meaning of the cross just as the cross illumines their meaning. In the opening chapter of the gospel John the Baptist, on seeing Jesus, proclaims, "Here is the lamb of God who takes away the sin of the world." Whatever else we may say of the cross it clearly must be about taking away the sin of the world, not adding to it. Any understanding of the cross that adds to the sin of the world cannot be legitimate.

The medieval crusaders' understanding of the cross as something in the name of which one must do battle is far from the glory that takes away the sin of the world. Neither can one simply find affirmation of the cross in the notion that the glory of the cross is in just taking it. There is no taking of abuse that can appeal to the cross as something glorious. This seems to be the fundamental error of the Mel Gibson movie, *The Passion of the Christ*. The ability to take it and be able to come back for more seems to run through many of his movies. Perhaps there is a glory in that but not the glory of the cross.

Jesus' prayer is for the fundamental unity of the church to be found in its comprehension of Jesus' glory. Clearly, in the gospel that glory focuses on the cross, yet that understanding must arise out of a correlation between the cross and the events of Jesus' life. When that happens, doors open to the taking away of the sin of the world.

Application

Ernest Campbell, in his sermon, "Locked in a Room with Open Doors," gives a laundry list of what the locks are in people's lives as they face the opportunities that surround them: worry, hatred, fear of the new. "The enemies are not all out there. Some are on the inside. It is so easy to fall into the habit of blaming our unrealized selves on outside forces. The mood of the day might well be caught up in a paraphrase of one of Shakespeare's better known lines, 'The fault, dear Brutus, is not in ourselves, but in our systems that we are miserable.' " Yet, what is on the inside also pushes us to needless activity.

What prompts feverish actions and all-too-frenetic activity on my part is: a mentor pastor that I do not want to let down, plain old-fashioned guilt, the inability to handle silence, and general anxiety as to what is coming next. These texts challenge me to consider whether in the next phase of my life I should yield to my drives or consider that it is God's plan for me to stay put, whether in my frenzied activity I have become a gatekeeper, and whether I seek to justify my theology more by action than reflection.

An Alternative Application
Revelation 22:12-14, 16-17, 20-21. One approach that I have found helpful is to consider my own history with a text. I often ask myself whether I have crossed any thresholds in reflecting on a text through the years. Increasingly, I find myself pondering the questions I find myself asking of a text. Years ago, I would not have asked the question of whether a text helped to break or add to cycles of violence. As one who does believe very much that the rule of God is about justice, I have found myself asking, "Where is the shadow side of this kind of preaching?"

Increasingly, I find that I ponder how the text will impact on other faith traditions and how doors to new meaning might be opened through that conversation. These texts measure my pilgrimage in terms of prisoners released, people free to enter the New Jerusalem, and the glory that Jesus intends for his people.

About the Authors

Wayne Brouwer teaches Religion, Theology, and Ministry Studies at both Hope College and Western Theological Seminary in Holland, Michigan. He holds degrees from Dordt College (A.B.), Calvin Theological Seminary (M.Div., Th.M.), and McMaster University (M.A., Ph.D.), and spent three decades as a pastor and international missionary teacher. Along with hundreds of published articles, Wayne Brouwer has authored thirteen books, including *Covenant Documents: Reading the Bible Again for the First Time* (Cognella), *The Literary Development of John 13-17: A Chiastic Reading* (SBL), and *Being a Believer in an Unbelieving World* (Hendrickson).

Timothy B. Cargal currently serves as Associate for Preparation for Ministry with the General Assembly of the Presbyterian Church (USA). For some twenty years he combined pastoral ministry with teaching biblical studies in universities and seminaries. He is the author of two books, including *Hearing a Film, Seeing a Sermon: Preaching and Popular Movies* (Westminster John Knox Press), and has contributed to several other books, study bibles, dictionaries, and journals in the areas of New Testament studies and preaching. He holds a Ph.D. in Religious Studies from Vanderbilt University.

David Kalas is the pastor of First United Methodist Church in Green Bay, Wisconsin. Before moving to Green Bay, he pastored churches in Whitewater, Wisconsin; Appleton, Wisconsin; and Hurt, Virginia. He also led youth ministries in Cleveland, Ohio, and Richmond, Virginia. David earned his undergraduate degree from the University of Virginia in Charlottesville and his Master of Divinity degree from Union Theological Seminary in Richmond, Virginia. He has also done coursework at Pittsburgh Theological Seminary and Asbury Theological Seminary.

In addition to the present volume, David has also contributed to other preaching resources published by CSS, is a regular contributor to *Emphasis: A Lectionary Preaching Journal* (CSS Publishing Company, Inc.), and has also written curriculum materials for the United Methodist Publishing House. David and his wife, Karen, have been married nearly 30 years and have three daughters, Angela, Lydia, and Susanna.

The late **R. Craig MacCreary** was pastor of South Congregational Church, United Church of Christ in Newport, New Hampshire. He held pastorates in Pennsylvania, West Virginia, and Massachusetts. He earned degrees from Elon University (B.A.), Lancaster Theological Seminary (M. Div.), and Hartford Seminary (D. Min.). His work appeared in *Colleague, Pulpit Digest*, and *The United Church News*. He was a guest on National Public Radio and was a contributor to *Candles in the Dark: Preaching and Poetry in Times of Crises*, edited by James Randolph.

Mark Molldrem has served as a pastor in the Evangelical Lutheran Church in America for 37 years. He has had parishes in Cobb/Edmund, Wisconsin; Beaver Dam, Wisconsin; Mondovi/Modena, Wisconsin; and Saginaw, Michigan. Currently he is Senior Pastor at First Lutheran Church in Beaver Dam, Wisconsin. Molldrem has written previously for CSS. He has authored numerous articles in various national magazines and journals. He received his Master of Divinity and also his Doctor of Ministry degrees from Luther Theological Seminary, St. Paul, Minnesota. He is very involved in his community, supporting People Against a Violent Environment (domestic violence) and developing community leadership through the Chamber of Commerce. Throughout the years, he has enjoyed art glass, martial arts, landscaping, preaching and teaching in the Lutheran Church in Liberia (West Africa), playing with his grandchildren, and vacationing with his wife, Shirley, with whom he has raised two children.